'*The Vibrant Organisation* takes the science & stories of creating vibrant organisations and converts them into a playbook of practical steps any leader can use. An essential read'.

—**Neil Munn**, *Global CEO, Bartle Bogle Hegarty.*

'*The Vibrant Organisation* provides a rigorous, evidence-based analysis of the neuroscientific and psychological states fundamental to engagement, productivity and development at work; it forges a missing link in business science'.

—**Adrian Webb**, *former Board Director, Gocompare,*
and co-founder of Adeki Performance.

'Very occasionally a book is written that actually has something fresh, valuable and easily accessible, to add to the world of human development in the business context, and this is undoubtedly one of those books. To not read it it is to miss out on the chance to bring to life your and your peoples best selves. If you want to leave a meaningful legacy, and be remembered for all the right reasons, put the clear, simple principles and practices of this book into action'.

—**Jeremy Sweeny**, *executive and team coach, working*
with some of the world's most senior leadership teams.

'A book of substance, style, and simplicity that provides todays leaders with a practical neuroscientific framework from which to build cultures of genuine excellence and well-being. A must read for any leader of any team or any organisation'.

—**George Karseras**, *CEO of TeamUp and author* of Build Better
Teams: Creating Winning Teams in the Digital Age.

'I highly recommend Duncan's powerful storytelling to all leaders across the globe grappling with changing culture by tapping into what cannot be found on a spreadsheet – the power of human potential'.

—**Jackie Gittins**, *CEO, Coach Nudge.*

T0383440

The Vibrant Organisation

The Vibrant Organisation translates the science of human behaviour into a playbook of highly practical interventions that build and scale enthusiasm, transforming organisational culture and performance. The book helps create more joy and fulfilment at work, whilst also steering a path to sustained competitive advantage.

Using cutting-edge research in neuroscience and psychology, as well as the author's considerable practical experience, Duncan Wardley offers a three-part framework for building teams of agile, adaptable, curious, and highly motivated people:

- *Reset* shows how to reduce the threat response by creating a safe environment for employees.
- *Ignite* teaches leaders how to create events or experiences that generate flashes of insight and motivation.
- *Fuel* demonstrates how to sustain people's motivation through repeatable actions, resulting in an upward spiral of enthusiasm.

Packed with fascinating research, on-the-ground stories, and new scientific findings – along with practical tools and exercises – *The Vibrant Organisation* is a must-read for business leaders at all levels looking to get the best out of themselves and their people.

Duncan Wardley has 25 years of practical experience helping to transform cultures at large organisations. He is the founder of Emote Consulting Limited, a company that uses the science of positive psychology to unleash the enthusiasm of individual leaders, teams, and organisations in service of their goals. Previously, Duncan was a partner at Heidrick & Struggles and led teams of cultural change specialists at both PwC and KPMG. Duncan lives with his family in Surrey, UK.

The Vibrant Organisation

*The Science of Scaling Enthusiasm
to Transform Performance*

Duncan Wardley

Routledge
Taylor & Francis Group

LONDON AND NEW YORK

Designed cover image: © Getty Images

First published 2024
by Routledge
4 Park Square, Milton Park, Abingdon, Oxon OX14 4RN

and by Routledge
605 Third Avenue, New York, NY 10158

Routledge is an imprint of the Taylor & Francis Group, an informa business

British Library Cataloguing-in-Publication Data
A catalogue record for this book is available from the British Library

Library of Congress Cataloging-in-Publication Data
Names: Wardley, Duncan, author.
Title: The vibrant organisation : the science of scaling enthusiasm to
    transform performance / Duncan Wardley.
Description: Abingdon, Oxon ; New York, NY : Routledge, 2024. |
    Includes bibliographical references and index. | Summary: "The Vibrant
    Organisation translates the science of human behaviour into a playbook
    of highly practical interventions that build and scale enthusiasm,
    transforming organisational culture and performance. The book helps
    create more joy and fulfilment at work, whilst also steering a path to
    sustained competitive advantage"—Provided by publisher.
Identifiers: LCCN 2023009005 | ISBN 9781032500874 (hardback) |
    ISBN 9781032500843 (paperback) | ISBN 9781003396833 (ebook)
Subjects: LCSH: Corporate culture | Psychology. | Human behavior.
Classification: LCC HM791 .W37 2024 | DDC 302.3/5—dc23/
    eng/20230309
LC record available at https://lccn.loc.gov/2023009005

ISBN: 978-1-032-50087-4 (hbk)
ISBN: 978-1-032-50084-3 (pbk)
ISBN: 978-1-003-39683-3 (ebk)

DOI: 10.4324/9781003396833

Typeset in Optima
by Apex CoVantage, LLC

For Tessa, with love and enthusiasm

Contents

Contents

Foreword

In the five years since I wrote *Alive at Work*, there has been a world-wide increase in leaders wanting to understand how to restore our zest for work. I believe three factors are at play here. First, the Covid pandemic has brought into sharp focus the need to address employee well-being, resilience, and motivation to better support (as well as attract and retain) staff. Second, the increasing interest in neuroscience in the business community has helped leaders to understand that if innovation and creativity are needed for long-term performance, then this is best achieved by activating employees' seeking systems, enabling them to have their best impact on the world. Third, there has been an encouraging societal shift, one where leaders have recognised the power of purpose in organisations, and have become more motivated to help their people live their lives to the fullest. In addition to the happiness bump that leaders themselves receive when they see the positive impact they can have on their staff, they find their workforce becomes more enthusiastic. The result is teams of people that work with conviction and creativity to solve the organisation's problems, while also improving team dynamics, retention rate, and employee health, as well as the organisation's bottom line.

For years, leaders have been saying that "employees are our most valuable asset." It seems they are now really starting to believe it. *Alive at Work* offered people a different way of looking at the world and has inspired many leaders to change. *The Vibrant Organisation* offers a useful, validated recipe of strategies and tools for what to do next – a practical approach for moving things forward. This is why Duncan has been one of the most popular guest lecturers in my classes over the last decade: He has made practical application of the scientific principles of positive psychology into his life's work.

Another factor that makes this work so timely is its focus on scale. Many self-help books exist that provide science-backed strategies for improving your joy and fulfilment at work. Few, if any, focus on how leaders can scale that engagement across their whole team, department, or organisation. This is because seeking system activation continues to be dampened by organisational systems and behaviours that value control and predictability over inspiration and creativity. This presents a still untapped opportunity for organisations to create vibrant organisations for the long term. *The Vibrant Organisation* presents strategies, tools, and examples that enable leaders to ignite their own seeking systems, and then those of their people. The system-wide approach is based in both science and practice and follows a sequence that can be applied at individual, team, and organisational levels.

I am confident that this book will prove to be an invaluable resource to leaders looking for a systematic and proven approach to creating environments that are full of purpose, where employees can experiment and express themselves. Leaders want the innovation, resilience, and superior business performance that come with this type of organisation. Applying the mindsets and behaviours detailed in these pages will let leaders experience an exhilarating and meaningful leadership journey and help organisations to become more Vibrant.

By Dan Cable, Professor of Organisational Behaviour,
London Business School

Acknowledgements

Friends, family, colleagues, clients, and academics have all been generous with their time as I tested the ideas, strategies, and methods in this book, and how they were written up and presented.

Special thanks to Professor Dan Cable for first introducing me to the "seeking system" and the world of positive psychology with all its possibilities to create truly vibrant organisations. Also for his help and encouragement in writing this field guide. I hope it does some justice to his research and writing.

To all my clients, colleagues, and collaborators, past and present, who have been both encouraging and challenging when needed – a perfect combination. Collectively you have stimulated enough ideas and content for another three books at least! To Adrian Webb, Neil Munn, Michael Parke, Jeremy Sweeney, Mary Puddepha, Anna Cleland, Sharon Sands, Adam Howe, Joe Anthamatten, TA Mitchell, Jackie Gittins, Glen Wallis, Bruce Daisley, Mark Dawson, Richard Crofton, Gill Ereaut, Zana Van de Ar, Andrew Wright, Marcus Thornley, Carl Hassan, David Lancefield, Richard Hytner, Lazlo Bock, and many others.

Thanks to Gina Almond for believing in the book and introducing me to my publisher Routledge. Also to Zoe Thomson, my editor, as well as Maddie Gray, Kevin Evers, and Zach Gajewski, who all played their part getting the manuscript in shape.

Finally to my family, Tessa, Anousha, Thea, Poppy, and Lottie. For doing what families do – keeping my seeking system fully fuelled when the twists and turns of this writing project threatened to raise my anxiety and overwhelm my cognitive load! Without you this book would never be out in the world.

Introduction

Terry loved his job. Charming and inspirational, he was a driven, performance-oriented leader who had risen to become country Head of Retail at a major multinational. Terry oversaw 400-plus stores and was responsible for a network of regional, area, and store managers. As with any retail enterprise, keeping track of the numbers was critical, and Terry watched them like a hawk. He had an almost encyclopaedic knowledge of sales figures, foot traffic, inventory turnover, gross margin, and other metrics. So when one of his flagship destination stores – let's call it store F – was consistently ranking as the worst sales performer, he knew something had to be done.

Terry and his leadership team dove into the data, trying to find clues that could help boost the store's performance. Nothing obvious stood out. The store manager was committed, the customer service strategy worked well across the network, they stocked market-leading products, and the store itself was well maintained and had good footfall (the number of customers entering a store over a given time period).

Terry knew that one of the biggest drivers of sales was the quality of the customer experience, which was highly impacted by the motivation and resulting behaviours of the in-store sales advisors. He had a hunch that this motivation could be the key to supercharging the store's performance. So, rather than implement new sales processes and systems, or demand better performance and exert more control, Terry decided to to take a risk. He would cede control to the front line.

The store was open Monday through Saturday, making it difficult to bring the staff together on any given day. After discussing options, the team agreed to give up a Sunday – for which they would get a day off in the following

DOI: 10.4324/9781003396833-1

weeks – so they could spend an entire day together discussing what was going on and how to improve their store's performance.

Terry employed a consulting firm to facilitate the session. They ran a series of exercises designed to connect everyone with their personal dreams, employing guided meditation, storytelling, and visualisation. Then, they shared them in a non-judgmental environment, giving them the confidence to speak openly and freely. Participants were encouraged to act on their life dreams by building a step-by-step plan to achieve them. Having explored their personal goals, next, the team ran an exercise to build a shared goal for the whole store. By discussing what they saw as the underlying purpose of the organisation and store, the team was able to identify key goals and actions needed to achieve them. Resources were explicitly made available to help them reach these goals, including visual marketing, merchandising, in-store-technology, project management, and self and team development support. They were energised by the exercise, and the group proceeded to develop a shared goal and action plan for the store, planning out what steps would be taken immediately and over the next month.

Most importantly, the employees were empowered to express themselves, both during the workshop and when they returned to the store. With a nominal budget, they were offered the chance to experiment with changes to the store and the way they interacted with customers and each other. Many threw away their company name badges. They re-wrote them with a one-liner of their personal dreams to engage their customers in a different type of conversation. One employee had written that his dream was to "make a living blogging," which opened up conversations about what he liked writing about and where his ideas came from, which were often a result of his interactions in the store. These dreams grabbed customers' attention as they were invited in to learn more about the employees and be given insight into who they are. These tag lines showed vulnerability and enabled deeper social connections, rather than strictly transactional ones.

Other employees decided to put "Hollywood Makeup Mirrors" at the back of the store so they could prepare themselves to look, feel, and be at their best before they walked "on stage" in the front of the store. More generally, by being given a chance to express themselves, employees saw meaning in their work in a way that had never occurred before.

In terms of revenue, store F jumped from last amongst destination stores to second place. In fact, the only other store doing better was the flagship store, with twice the floor space and footfall. All the other retail outlets heard about what was going on; energy at store F had been unleashed and leaders throughout the network wanted to understand how it had happened and why it was so successful. Many employees even wanted to transfer to what people within the company were now calling "The Dream Store."

What It Means to Be a Vibrant Organisation

At a neurological level, it is fairly certain that during the initial workshop, and in the months that followed, the employees at the Dream Store activated a part of their brain referred to as the "seeking system." A core component of the central reward system in the brain, when triggered, the seeking system – or ventral striatum – releases the neurotransmitter dopamine. Dopamine is an *enthusiasm maker*, and in this situation, it helped lead to higher workforce engagement and creativity.

When leaders systematically trigger employees' seeking systems and help employees pursue what they really want from their careers and their lives, organisations become more vibrant. A vibrant organisation is one where leaders help their people live their lives to the fullest, and in return, receive the benefits that only a fully energised organisation can. It's what we *all* want: a personal sense of purpose, opportunities for ongoing learning and growth, and the chance to do what we do best every day. By transforming their organisation into a vibrant one, leaders can turn their workforce into a volunteer army that works with conviction, enthusiasm, and creativity to solve the organisation's problems, while improving team dynamics, retention rate, creative problem solving, employee satisfaction and health, and the organisation's bottom line. Or in other words – true success.

It's not an easy dream to realise. But my 20-plus years helping clients to create effective positive cultural and behavioural change has led me to a heartening conclusion: whole organisations *can* become more vibrant, to the benefit of both employers and employees. Understanding the triggers of the seeking system is critical, but the secret lies in learning some of the practical tools, strategies, and methodologies, the sequence in which they should be applied, and the key principles and steps behind scaling human potential.

In 2018, Professor Dan Cable's book *Alive at Work* explored how the neurological seeking system could be activated at work. He showed how stimulating the triggers of self-expression, experimentation, and personalised purpose – within a defined operational framework – enables employees to bring more of their full potential to the workplace. When employees' seeking systems are triggered, leaders get more energy and innovation from the workforce than they would have ever expected. This is exactly what happened at the Dream Store.[1]

These three triggers manifest in the following ways:

- **Self-expression** relates to our desire to use our unique skills, share our perspectives, and make our own decisions. Research shows that when we think about and use our strengths, our seeking systems are activated and we feel more alive. At the Dream Store, encouraging employees to express their life dreams and explore how their work could help them on that path activated self-expression.
- **Experimentation** unleashes intrinsic motivations and creativity. Experimental "safe zones" at work can include play, practice, and supportive social bonding. Firms also become more agile when they encourage employees to think up and try out new ways of doing things, and then get feedback about how their stakeholders responded to their ideas. Experimentation was built into the Dream Store intervention as employees were encouraged to experiment with their own ideas without fear of negative consequences.
- **Personalised Purpose** is ignited when we can see the cause and effect between our actions and their outcomes. At work, we feel a sense of purpose when we can experience first-hand how our contributions help other people and allow our co-workers and customers to thrive. Purpose works best when employees get to interact directly with the people they are affecting with their work, and this was also true for the Dream Store employees. The immediate feedback they received from customers helped their sense of purpose soar.

To activate these three triggers, team members need to be supported. Great organisations balance a strong sense of employee freedom and experimentation within an *operational frame*. The frame refers to how organisations need employees to meet regulations, deliver on promises to customers, and follow key operational processes. When the tension between the freedom and the frame is just right, employees' enthusiasm and ideas are directed toward solving organisational problems. Work feels more meaningful to employees, and organisations get the creativity and innovation that keeps them relevant.

At the Dream Store, employees were also afforded freedom within a frame. While they were encouraged to experiment with ideas, there were some well-defined limits, such as a maximum (and modest) capital spend for any store changes. "Install a hologram to greet customers at a cost of $200,000" would have been outside the operational frame. Employees understood the desired results, the available resources, the rules they had to follow, and the routines and systems they could work with. Importantly, though, they were given the freedom needed to experiment and self-express in service of their purpose.

But, somewhat unfortunately, that's not the end of the Dream Store story.

The Importance of Scale

In this real-life case, over-zealous executives tried to harvest the ideas from the Dream Store employees and apply them across all other retail outlets: "Let's put makeup mirrors in all the stores!" This makes sense, logically – take what worked at one store and apply it to the others. As you might have guessed, however, this rational approach completely missed the point. The value was not in the specific ideas (makeup mirrors) but in the zest, enthusiasm, and engagement that was unleashed when employees' seeking systems were activated. These positive emotions failed to materialise when other retail outlets were instructed to implement ideas that had not been created by their people, void of their own self-expression, experimentation, or personalised purpose.

To be blunt, when people don't feel meaning or ownership behind an initiative, their seeking systems will not be activated. In many cases, Hollywood makeup mirrors are more likely to invite cynicism and scepticism than joy if they appear in the break room one day without explanation. A dilemma emerges: leaders want the enthusiasm and creativity of their staff, but they also want the efficiencies of standardisation, simplification, and control. If every store was allowed to do things their own way, what would happen to the brand identity? What about stores' operational costs?

This conflict shows why efforts to scale engagement are so difficult. It's difficult enough to provide the leadership support and organisational freedom to allow a small number of employees in a team to "do things differently." But things get really tough when leaders try to generate engagement across the *whole organisation*. The rational logic of rollouts just doesn't apply when it comes to activating positive emotions, but many leaders have not yet learned or practiced the *emotional* activation needed to create agility at scale. So the question becomes: What are the practical steps needed to create the level of energy and success seen in the Dream Store? And how can this be translated to *all* of the stores? Most importantly, how can it be translated to *your* organisation so it can become more vibrant?

Throughout this book, you'll find a blend of scientific evidence, practical strategies and tools, and real-life examples from leaders and organisations who have embarked on this journey and found success in the process. Every piece of advice is backed by experience and scientific evidence, all of which includes references in case you want to read the fine print in more detail. The purpose of the book is to translate this science into practical, step-by-step techniques for helping more of your employees feel a zest for their life and work.

Structure and Core Concepts

The Vibrant Organisation has four main parts:

- **Part 1**, Science Essentials, shares the science and principles of both individual and scaled emotional transformation, providing a look into the mindset *you* need to lead your organisation's vibrant transformation. Being a vibrant organisation is an *emotional* transformation, one that simply cannot be injected into an organisation if your own seeking system is not activated.

    Parts 2, 3, and 4 are structured around an emerging theory of change based on the idea of "self-directed neuroplasticity," which suggests that it is *attention itself* that effectively re-wires the brain and causes us to think differently.[2] So by focusing on a new idea or behaviour in just the right way, for just the right amount of time, we create new neural connections – literally changing the way we think.

This type of change requires a three-step sequence of activities, called Reset, Ignite, and Fuel. This sequence can be applied at an individual or an organisational level to facilitate seeking system activation, with each step forming the remaining parts of the book.

- **Part 2** is called Reset. When people are experiencing fear, anxiety, or overwhelm at work, it is all but impossible to ignite their seeking systems. The first step to becoming a vibrant organisation is to reduce cognitive load, regulate emotion, and create "psychological safety" for your employees to experiment with new approaches to work.[3] This section explores surprising strategies for resetting yourself, your team, and your entire organisation.

- **Part 3** is called Ignite. Ignition is about creating those light-bulb moments of insight that make us re-think the way we view the world. At a moment of insight, a complex set of new neural connections is being created. These "Ah-ha" moments can provide clarity of direction and a burst of wide-eyed enthusiasm. Igniting your people's seeking system therefore requires recognising, encouraging, and deepening your team's flashes of insight as the rush of insight is strengthened if they go through the process of making new neural connections themselves. This section explains how to cultivate moments of insight and ignite the seeking system at scale.

- **Part 4** is called Fuel. Once new neural circuits, or patterns of thought, have been formed, they need to be given repeated attention in order for them to stay alive, eventually resulting in new habits. One needs to apply hard work and consistent effort to achieve any form of positive change. This section will provide strategies for maintaining new behaviours until they become habitual.

The reset, ignite, fuel cycle is sequential, so it is best to read the book in the order it is presented to get a strong sense of what is required to create a truly vibrant organisation. The book can then act as a guide as you navigate your own transformation; you can dip into specific chapters when you want details on tools and strategies relevant to the stage in which your organisation finds itself.

With that all said, let's dive in.

Notes

1 Dan Cable and I have known and worked together for more than a decade, and his research has been central to informing my consulting approach. For those who want to learn more about the seeking system triggers, I wholly endorse his book and recommend you read it.

2 Doidge, Norman (2007) *The Brain That Changes Itself: Stories of Personal Triumph from the Frontiers of Brain Science*. London, England: Penguin.

3 Edmondson, Amy C. (2018) *The Fearless Organization: Creating Psychological Safety in the Workplace for Learning, Innovation, and Growth*. Hoboken, New Jersey: John Wiley & Sons.

PART 1

The Essential Science of Scale

The Science of Positive Change

Bruce Daisley sat there – in the London office on Great Titchfield Street – worried. When he was hired as the general manager of Twitter EMEA (Europe, Middle East, and Africa), poached from his former position at Google, he arrived in the UK in January 2012 to find a group of 15 people, and another 500 globally, all tethered to the beat of Silicon Valley. The HQ team back in San Francisco was not used to working with a new team in a different country, and Bruce's smart and motivated group was locked into the "unfortunate gravitational pull of headquarters."

As Bruce described it, each day the team would come up with great solutions to local problems they were facing, but they felt the need to request permission to pursue them. Given the time lag of eight hours on the West Coast, whenever Bruce's UK team pitched ideas to the folks in San Francisco, it was as if they were hollering into a deep valley. It was not until the next day they would hear the echo coming back from California. And when the response finally arrived from HQ, the answer was often "No." As in, "No, you're not allowed to pursue that idea." "No, you can't use your budget that way." "No, that idea is not entirely consistent with our brand."

After more of the same, week in and week out, this approach became debilitating and demotivating. While well-intentioned, HQ leaders did not understand the local conditions, and each negative response demoralised the UK team a little more. Learned helplessness started settling in. Rather than "playing to win," the UK team fell into a style of permission-based working that made them "play not to lose." The result: a smart group of talented people was pedalling excruciatingly slowly when they needed to be driving hard and pivoting fast, as they were up against competitors like Facebook.

DOI: 10.4324/9781003396833-3

The team was also fighting limited exposure in the UK. By the time Bruce joined Twitter EMEA, it was common in California to see the blue bird logo on menus in restaurants and hear hashtags mentioned by DJs on the radio. In London, however, this was not the case. Twitter was just starting to emerge, with a few quirky, intelligent celebrities using it. It lacked the fizz that One Direction and Justin Bieber later brought to it. Hashtags were not yet "a thing" in the UK, and Twitter was overlooked as a social media force in London – it seemed small, niche, and irrelevant. The London team had been tasked with getting Twitter noticed, and fast.

Bruce is both an inspiring leader and an expert in workplace culture (check out his best-selling books *The Joy of Work* and *Fortitude*, plus his podcast *Eat, Sleep, Work, Repeat*). He knew he had to create an environment where his employees would not feel constrained and anxious. To start, they first needed a clear understanding of both the UK team goals and of the real (not assumed) rules and regulations within which they should work. Working within this operational frame, as discussed in the Introduction, they then needed to be given the freedom to use their own initiative and to continually challenge the frame. To do this, he instigated a simple rule. He called it "Blame Bruce."

Bruce told his team "Within these constraints, use your own initiative. And if it doesn't work out, I've got your back. Just Blame Bruce." This small idea created a *huge* change. Here's how Bruce put it: "I didn't call it a philosophy or anything august. I just used to say "your idea sounds good to me, let's try it. Look, if anyone pulls you up on it, just tell them I made you do it. Blame me. BLAME BRUCE! Everyone listen: that goes for you too, just blame me. I can handle it."

The Blame Bruce policy was a bit of fun: light, easy to remember, and energising. But it also was meaningful. In fact, it reflected his personal worldview. "I've always worked under the philosophy that 'we're all going to be fired one day,'" said Bruce. "None of us wants to go through our whole career more worried about being fired than doing something cool. And when I describe how I got fired, I'd much rather tell a story where I was proud of what we were working on." He wanted that story to emphasise what they aimed to accomplish, even if not all their goals were achieved. "A story when we were energized, we had fun, and tried to accomplish great things. I don't want to go down saying 'we didn't accomplish much, but we sure didn't break any rules.'"

With the Blame Bruce policy, teams started acting on their own clever ideas, without feeling like they needed to wait to hear the echo from the Silicon Valley canyon. They began taking personal initiatives with, and ownership over, the projects. Bruce saw his team become much more focused, putting fresh ideas into their work. He also noticed that their internal work was more inventive, with employees bringing more personality to their presentation slides and presenting fun new ideas. They didn't seem as if they were just "going through the motions of a job."

He watched with pride as the UK Twitter team attacked the market, working like mavericks to get the logos everywhere: featured on TV shows, used by football teams, and printed on the menus at cafés and bars. Bruce's brief to the marketing leader had been "just go create lots of reasons for people to pull their phones out of their pockets and take pictures." The team hosted events that projected mystique, filling pubs with musicians, comedians, and influencers who brought their friends along just for the fun. They got street artists to use hashtags, and they signed up unconventional speakers at their events. With "#Twitter" being prominently featured on posters and signs at these gatherings, the company gained attention every time they succeeded in motivating people that attended to take pictures and share them with their friends.

The London offices' clients started noticing Twitter "out in the wild," and in response, gave them more opportunities to present to their teams. Clients also increasingly included Twitter hashtags in their own work. One called Bruce to tell him "I loved your team's presentation this week, it picked up our own team. When they finished, we actually wanted more of it." Another told him, "We've started putting the Twitter presentations at the very beginning of our meetings, because they're the most engaging for our own team."

Of course, not every initiative or project was a big hit, and people sometimes did, in fact, "blame Bruce." For example, one team member created a rather wild, irreverent book called #TheMoment. The point was to show a wide audience how Twitter was changing communication. On the upside, loads of influential people loved the book, and it generated serious buzz. #TheMoment featured gritty pictures – and content – hand-written and drawn by the UK Twitter team, which received a lot of attention. On the downside, when that attention made its way to HQ, leaders were reticent. They had not seen anything like it before. One picture showed hashtags in the shape of Margaret Thatcher's nose (who had died that year). Another was of a man tweeting while sitting on the toilet. The book was eye-catching, raw, and political. HQ said it was way too edgy and inconsistent with the Twitter brand.

Both the book in general and some particular images pushed too hard on the frame in which employees had to work as part of the Twitter culture. A number of senior leaders wanted to put processes in place to avoid such a thing from happening again. Others, like the German team, loved it so much they sent a full translation to print for their market. True to his word, Bruce took the heat for the book and other "oversights." He discussed the situation with HQ and stood by his employees, claiming he knew full well about the book, its style, and its intent. In the end, Bruce agreed with the top brass that it was a step too far outside brand regulations. It was an awkward hour, to be sure, but from Bruce's perspective, you need to be ready to take a little heat now and again if you want employees taking initiative and experimenting in the spirit of helping the organisation. #TheMoment was not mean-spirited and certainly was not wilful damage, so Bruce was happy to take the blame.

Through the Blame Bruce policy, Bruce had managed to activate his team's seeking system by focusing on the seeking system triggers. What is equally interesting, however, is the sequence of activities that he put in place to achieve this – resetting the UK team's environment, igniting their creativity, and fuelling their sustained efforts. To understand this reset, ignite, fuel sequence in more detail, and how it can be applied both personally and in larger settings, we must first explore the underlying neuroscience of change that causes its effectiveness.

The Neuroscience of Change

While many scientists and medical professionals in the early twentieth century believed the neural structure of the human brain to be fixed in place, the current consensus in the field of neuroscience offers an opposing view. We now recognise that the brain has the capacity to change its structure by creating new neural connections and pathways in response to different sensory experiences.

This change occurs through a process known as self-directed neuroplasticity (SDN). Simply put, when you redirect your attention, you facilitate SDN,[1] in which your new focus creates new neural pathways, literally changing the way your brain works, the way you think, and your habits. The idea is that *focused attention* effectively rewires the brain and causes us to think differently.[2] Foundational work by psychiatrist Jeffrey Schwarz has defined SDN as "using the power of focused attention, along with the ability to apply commitment, hard work, and dedication, to direct your choices and actions, thereby rewiring your brain to work for you."

Neurons are the nerve cells that form our brain circuitry, while a synapse is the tiny gap between neurons that functionally links them together. These synaptic connections help build the linkages that become the unique scaffolding of the brain. The brain is dynamic, constantly changing its synaptic connections in response to experiences, and creating networks of billions of connected neurons as unique as an individual fingerprint. It is this circuitry that helps us store memories, create emotional reactions, initiate thought processes, and produce action.

Neurons transmit signals to each other through an electrical impulse; when this happens, they are said to be "firing." Repetitive firing along the same neural pathways within the brain creates stronger neural connections and organisation. As neuropsychologist Donald Hebb puts it, "Neurons that fire together, wire together."[3] And focused attention on a thought, idea, or behaviour causes many brain regions to synchronously fire together. The more a network of neurons fire together, the more that network becomes hardwired in the brain. Hebb's law dictates that as nerve cells repeatedly activate, it becomes easier for them to fire in unison. Over time, whatever thought, behaviour, or feeling that results from this repeated nerve cell activation becomes an automatic, unconscious habit.

One striking example of SDN at work is found in London taxi drivers. All London taxi drivers are required to have a detailed knowledge of London within a six-mile radius of Charing Cross, the official centre of the city and the point to which all distances to the nation's capital are measured. Candidates have to memorise the world-renowned "Knowledge of London," a total of 320 routes that criss-cross London and are specifically designed to cover the 60,000-plus streets and over 100,000 places of note within the area. It takes a candidate between two to four years to master this knowledge.

Irish neuroscientist Eleanor Maguire and her colleagues conducted a study to test if London taxi drivers' brains changed as a result of this exceptional training. In particular, she investigated how extensive use of visuo-spatial memory (the ability to visualise where objects are in relation to each other) interacts with the development of the hippocampus, a part of the brain that effects learning and memory. In addition to being one of the most change-able, or plastic, sections of the brain, the hippocampus is responsible for visuo-spatial skills such as learning routes. Maguire showed that London taxi drivers have larger hippocampi, when compared to a control group, and that the longer the length of time an individual operates as a taxi driver, the greater his or her hippocampal volume.[4]

The Knowledge of London emphasises that what we pay attention to changes our brains. The bad news is that we tend to naturally pay attention to negative experiences above positive ones. When attempting to activate the seeking system, whether our own or others, this can be a serious prob-lem. As a means of survival, our brains evolved to heavily attune to the possibility of threat. While this is great as a survival strategy, it's not so great as a thriving strategy. There is a greater surge in the brain's electrical activity when faced with negative, rather than positive, stimuli. Psychologist and bestselling author Rick Hanson explains the situation as such: "The brain is like Velcro for negative experiences but Teflon for positive ones."[5] The neural circuitry emerging from repeated negativity bias risks becoming a serious burden on psychological well-being.

Over time, after many negative experiences, the brain sensitises to more negative experiences. As an example, Harvard psychologist David Levari showed people hundreds of images of faces and asked them to rate the pho-tos as threatening or non-threatening. As people saw more and more faces, Levari changed the ratio of scary-to-nice by putting in fewer threatening faces. As the subjects saw less threatening faces, their standards for what constituted a threatening face decreased, so eventually a look of neutrality was deemed "threatening."[6]

This propensity to focus on negative experiences is one reason why acti-vating the seeking system is so hard and why positive change is so difficult to implement across an organisation, or even within a team (or ourselves). As a leader, you are responsible for facilitating change across your team or organisation, but typically, when people feel as if you are trying to change them, their automatic threat response kicks in. Negativity bias tends to make us view change as a threat to our status or autonomy, rather than an excit-ing opportunity. What's more, the impact of a negative experience is often stronger than that of a positive one. This situation is a real double whammy – we not only look out for negative experiences, but those experiences have a greater impact on us. That means most of us, including leaders and their teams, instinctually resist change.

Psychologist Barbara Fredrickson at the University of North Carolina shows that the tipping point for the sort of high performance associated with seeking system activation comes only when we experience positive emotions in a 3-to-1 ratio to negative emotions.[7] Leaders must therefore work especially hard to enact change at scale. Ensuring a steady pulse of seeking system triggers that are frequent and ongoing to overwhelm any stimulus that can be interpreted as negative or threatening is no easy task.

That's where the reset, ignite, fuel sequence comes into play. To facilitate self-directed neuroplasticity in service of seeking system activation, this neurological sequence must be followed. Let's look at these steps in more detail while revisiting Bruce Daisly's story through the lens of self-directed neuroplasticity.

Reset

The seeking system is in a continual battle with another, extremely powerful, motivational system which can simply be called the "fear system." Fear is kryptonite to the seeking system. As we go about our daily life, we scan for threats and rewards that can trigger either system. The fear response originates from the amygdala, which assesses the emotional significance of things that happen in our environment, particularly whether or not something in that environment is a threat to us.

As stress hormones, like norepinephrine and cortisol, are released, the body prepares for "fight, flight, or freeze." Research shows that activating the fear system narrows cognitive processing as we focus in on removing the threat. In fact, it is hard to focus on anything else until that threat is sufficiently removed and we feel safe again. Though fear *can* provide energy and focus, it's a sure way to shut off curiosity and experimentation. Worse yet, the long-term activation of the stress response system and overexposure to cortisol and other stress hormones can disrupt almost all our bodies' processes, putting us at increased risk of long-term health problems. Fear also diminishes the quality of our thinking in the pre-frontal cortex, which is responsible for our complex cognitive processing such as planning, setting goals, and making decisions.

Unfortunately, many organisations are fear-based. After all, management is based on KPIs and metrics used to evaluate employees, and then managers motivate them by threatening loss of pay, promotion, job, and status for employees who don't meet the standards. When people experience fear, it is all but impossible to ignite their seeking systems. So, the first step in the neurobiology of change is to reduce the threat response by creating a safe environment for employees. "Psychological safety" is a prerequisite for employees to experiment with new approaches to work.[8] Most leaders must therefore trigger their employees' seeking system by first resetting, which will build a strong sense of belonging among employees, encourage their well-being, and develop psychological safety across the enterprise.

But to reset, we need to do more than regulate or reframe our emotional state. We also need to free up our working memory, which is plagued by endless e-mails, deadlines, meetings, projects, and proposals. To do so, we need to reduce our cognitive load through simplification, prioritisation, and organisation, enabling us space to focus on what matters most. Resetting will help us understand and simplify the framework within which we all operate.

Take Bruce Daisley. Bruce instinctively knew success lay in unleashing the creativity and enthusiasm of his UK Twitter team. His "Blame Bruce" rule provided a perfect form of reset as it created an environment that reduced the threat response his employees had felt from the stifling bureaucracy of HQ. Bruce also provided his team with permission to discuss and challenge assumptions around the operational frame they had to work within. He recognised that some rules were important but too many could be stifling.

Often, we instinctively know when we require a reset. We can feel when our psychological well-being diminishes, ultimately resulting in burnout. We become tired and stressed no matter how much sleep we get. We over-eat or under eat. We're grumpy and not much fun to be around at all. Every additional task seems overwhelming and never ending, Sisyphus rolling that boulder up the hill for all eternity. Whether we recognise it in ourselves, to our peers, or our team members, it's obvious to see, often written on our faces. We know when it's time for a reset. And by resetting at work, we can get out of this funk and prepare for the next stage of the cycle: ignite.

Ignite

Professor Mark Beeman of Northwestern University has used fMRI and EEG technologies to study moments of insight. One of his studies found that sudden bursts of high-frequency EEG activity, known as gamma waves, appear in the brain just prior to these very such moments[9]. As gamma waves represent cognitive processing in the brain (such as linking together different pieces of information), the findings suggest that during an insightful moment, a new network of neural connections is created. When you want to engage seeking systems, and change the way people think and behave, you need to recognise, encourage, and deepen their flashes of insight.

The more an insight is generated from within, rather than handed to us as conclusions, the more powerful it is. This idea may be inefficient but it is based on our biology: people experience more of a rush of insight if they go through the process of making new neural connections themselves. This moment of insight is a positive and energising experience, and that rush of energy is central to facilitating change – it helps fight against the amygdala's fear response that can hold us back.

So, large-scale behaviour change requires organic change in each employee's mental map. This, in turn, requires some kind of event or experience that allows people to provoke themselves into a flash of insight. As leaders, we need to help facilitate that event or experience (specific strategies are covered in Part 3). Doing so takes practice and skills that we may have never cultivated in any serious way in the past. For decades management meant control, metrics, and catching people doing things wrong. Management has been about removing uncertainty and trying to "fix mistakes," not ignite creativity and change. Because we are more likely to have creative insights when we can use our unique strengths in service of a higher purpose, the ignite step also requires helping individuals and teams to better understand their strengths, and to change the way they work to be at their best more often.

After a successful reset that created a safe environment for his employees, Bruce Daisly helped ignite his teams' seeking systems through a combination of setting challenges, asking questions, and rapid feedback loops to learn from experiences. "Just go create lots of reasons for people to pull their phone out of their pockets and take pictures" was just one such challenge that got the team excited and unleashed their potential.

Fuel

In seeking to conserve energy – a default survival strategy – the brain resists the formation of new neural connections in order to retain its current state. Therefore, we need to apply hard work and consistent effort to achieve any form of positive change. Once new neural circuits or patterns of thought have been formed, they need to be given repeated attention in order for them to stay alive, and eventually result in new habits. This repeated attention enables new brain circuitry to become established, which then develops into an intrinsic part of our identity. The amount of attention paid to a particular thought is called "attention density." Attention density can be increased by raising the frequency, intensity, or amplitude of attention.

With our seeking systems ignited, we can feel passionate and engaged in our work. To continue to fuel the seeking system, however, it's important that we embark on a journey to continually improve at what we do. Objective feedback that shows improvements in impact and performance provides us with a feeling of progress and purpose. And to improve at anything in life, we need to *practice new activities*. Unfortunately, the concept of practice is not embedded in many businesses. Businesspeople are so busy, they spend most of their time "performing" – trying to add value to the enterprise – rather than "practicing" to get better. If practice is encouraged, it is often reserved for short periods of learning new knowledge and skills, without a focus on continuous development.

The core purpose of any performance management process is to enable individuals and teams to perform at their best so they can achieve individual and organisational success. However, most of these processes were originally built using an industrial paradigm for predictable, repeatable environments, where people have clearly defined roles and responsibilities. Such approaches often place more emphasis on assessing performance (for the calculation and distribution of compensation, promotions, and the like) than actually improving it.

Addressing performance management and pay was something that Bruce Daisly employed to fuel the seeking systems of his Twitter team. He introduced group-based bonuses. Empirical evidence shows that individual bonuses are more likely to create divisiveness between employees as everyone looks out for himself or herself (a topic further explored in Chapter 10). According to Bruce, under individual-based incentives, employees were less likely to share reports, slides, and other important information or work. That's because individual incentives create a tournament where helping colleagues ends up hurting you when it comes to bonus time.

Even though Bruce understood the risks around social loafing – in which certain members of the team may slack and still get the benefits of their teammates' hard work – he felt team-based incentives fit the engaged culture, and he made bonuses pay out when the team hit certain targets. This was inconsistent with Twitter's corporate policies, and the company's West Coast executives were not happy about it. But in this case, Bruce prevailed and continued to use group-based bonuses as the UK team's performance soared. In the long run, Bruce's team-based approach to igniting employees' seeking systems helped the larger organisation grow by showing HQ that their assumptions about individual-based bonuses were questionable.

The Sequence in Action

You might already see how this model of reset, ignite, fuel is a fractal, a pattern that repeats across different scales. At an individual level, a person may pass through each step over the course of a 30-minute meeting or over the course of a two-year transformation program – or both. Likewise, the same pattern applies to short-term organisational issues (for example, a two-week experiment) as well as long term strategic changes (such as a full-on cultural change). For a quick example of the reset, ignite, fuel model in action on an Individual level, let's take a look at John, who is feeling stressed before a weekly sales meeting.

John's business unit is behind on its sales targets, and John knows he needs to be thinking clearly and creatively if the team are to accelerate performance. He is feeling anxious, but he needs his own seeking system engaged if he expects to model the curiosity and excitement his team need during the meeting.

Five minutes before the meeting John realises he needs to **reset**. He's already had a busy day with lots of new pressing issues. So, he reduces his cognitive load by writing down a list of the things he needs to deal with *after* the sales meeting, which helps him get the swirl of activity he's experiencing out of his head. He then simplifies the list by chunking related actions together and focusing only on the most critical elements. This simplified list calms John's anxiety (it's short, focused, and salient) and lets him focus his energies on the meeting, because once it's all written down, he can forget about it – he will deal with it after the sales meeting. He then undertakes a two-minute mindfulness exercise, getting himself to focus on the present and put all his attention on the sales meeting. Just prior to starting the meeting, he reduces all external distractions by switching off his mobile phone and disabling e-mail alerts. John knows that while each of these steps is small, together they make a powerful difference in the way he will process and respond to his environment.

To **ignite** his team in the meeting, John introduces a deliberate disruption to his team's established thinking patterns by suggesting a new seating plan. He also invites a colleague from within the organisation, but outside his team, to attend and provide an external perspective to the meeting. The colleague is asked to play the "role" of customer in the meeting, responding to the team's ideas as if he were a client. John further ignites his own seeking system – and that of his team – by framing the current sales gap as a challenge, an endeavour that will be interesting to work on and solve, not a threat looming over them all. By focusing on the *outcome* of achieving their sales target, John primes everyone's brains to focus on a goal they all desire, making the team receptive to the information most relevant to that outcome, rather than to focus on information about the problem itself. Focusing on the problem would only serve to activate the fear system – narrowing cognitive processing and inhibiting insights – making the team significantly less innovative.

The team generates a number of new ideas for a "guerrilla marketing" campaign that they think could significantly increase sales. With energy and excitement in the room high, the team creates an action plan, and people volunteer to drive different parts of the plan. Across the next week, John **fuels** that energy by providing enthusiastic recognition, sending around encouraging e-mails and giving shout-outs in team meetings to recognise individuals' work. He also makes it easier for his team to complete the action plan by prioritising this work, delaying some of their other commitments and delegating some to other employees. By delaying another project by two weeks, and bringing in temporary resources to complete some of the team's "business as usual" activity, they are able to give this challenge focused attention.

Summary

- Scaling enthusiasm in individuals, teams, and organisations requires frequent activation of the seeking system. This dopamine-producing brain system provides motivation through rewards and is triggered through a sense of personalised purpose, experimentation, and self-expression.
- For most people, frequently feeling the zest associated with seeking system activation requires some changes to the way they think and respond to their circumstances. This change can be facilitated through a process

of self-directed neuroplasticity (SDN). The idea is that *focused attention* effectively rewires the brain, causing us to think differently.

- Providing focused attention on seeking system activation is difficult due to people's propensity to focus on negative experiences (negativity bias). To achieve the benefits of seeking system activation, aim for a ratio of 3-to-1 of positive to negative experiences.
- SDN is facilitated through a repeating cycle, or fractal: reset (creating a safe environment and a clear focus); ignite (engineering experiences that allow people to provoke themselves into a flash of insight, changing their mental maps); and fuel (giving repeated attention to new thought patterns in order for them to stay alive, eventually resulting in new habits).

Notes

1 Schwartz, Jeffrey M., Henry P. Stapp, and Mario Beauregard (2005) Quantum physics in neuroscience and psychology: a neurophysical model of mind–brain interaction. *Philosophical Transactions of the Royal Society B: Biological Sciences* 360, no. 1458: 1309–1327.

2 Doidge, Norman (2007) *The Brain That Changes Itself: Stories of Personal Triumph from the Frontiers of Brain Science*. London, England: Penguin.

3 Hebb, Donald (2002) *The Organization of Behavior*. New York: Psychology Press.

4 Maguire, Eleanor A., Katherine Woollett, and Hugo J. Spiers (2006) "London taxi drivers and bus drivers: a structural MRI and neuropsychological analysis." *Hippocampus* 16, no. 12: 1091–1101.

5 Hanson, Rick (2013) *Hardwiring Happiness: The New Brain Science of Contentment, Calm, and Confidence*. New York: Harmony Books.

6 Levari, David E., Daniel T. Gilbert, Timothy D. Wilson, Beau Sievers, David M. Amodio, and Thalia Wheatley (2018) "Prevalence-induced concept change in human judgment." *Science* 360, no. 6396: 1465–1467.

7 Fredrickson, Barbara (2010) *Positivity – Groundbreaking Research to Release Your Inner Optimist and Thrive*. Oneworld Publications, Oxford, England.

8 Edmondson, Amy C. (2018) *The Fearless Organization: Creating Psychological Safety in the Workplace for Learning, Innovation, and Growth*. Hoboken, New Jersey: John Wiley & Sons.

9 Kounios, John, and Mark Beeman (2015) *The Eureka Factor: Aha Moments, Creative Insight, and the Brain*. London, England: Random House, p. 70.

2   Scaling the Sequence

Sales agents in Jeff Lee's financial software firm were consistently failing to meet performance targets. Jeff (real person, fake name) had long felt something was missing in the way the team operated, but he always struggled to fully articulate exactly what it was. He was frustrated at the work rate of some of his staff and also suspected that some team members' behaviours were more about "gaming the system" for their own personal benefit than doing the best they could for the customer. Desperate for improvements and hoping for some "secret sauce" that would motivate his team toward peak performance, Jeff sought assistance from a consulting firm.

The firm suggested an approach based on Lean Process Improvement, a continuous process of looking at value from the customer point of view, eliminating waste, and focusing on delivering what the customer needs when they need it. External coaches would work with Jeff's sales teams, 25 people at a time, over an intense 12-week period. Supported by a technical specialist who could provide workflow and data processing knowledge and KPIs, the team would spend that time learning about and embedding new ways of working into their sales process. The first pilot would include six teams.

The mere introduction of the 12-week program acted as a reset for the team due to what Katy Milkman, a professor of psychology at the Wharton School, calls the "fresh start effect." Milkman coined this term after her research found that people are most inclined to make meaningful changes around "temporal landmarks," those points in time naturally associated with a new beginning (think New Year's resolution).[1] Embarking on a well-defined, 12-week journey supported by a team of consultants created a psychological opportunity for change. This effect was then repeated during each week of the program.

    DOI: 10.4324/9781003396833-4

The reset, ignite, fuel sequence picked up from there. Every Monday morning, the coaches would reset by acknowledging progress to date and then introducing a new tool to each team leader – that would become the prime focus of the coming week. On Tuesday, the team leader would ignite the team by training them in the use of the tool. The team's seeking systems would continue to be fuelled for the remainder of that week by focused application of the tool. This process would be repeated every week so that, by the end of week 12, a new way of working would have been introduced and habituated.

The teams found the new tools and approaches helpful, but the coaches never introduced them as "the final answers" to the teams' problems. Instead, team members were encouraged to try out the tools and adapt them to their local issues, giving them insights into their effectiveness and increasing their feelings of ownership over their performance (ignite).

Teams also tested the new tools and practices in their day-to-day activities at work, rather than passively learning about them in a controlled setting. This real-time active participation allowed the new behaviours to be practiced daily (fuel). The coaches provided rapid feedback on daily operational performance by placing physical screens and whiteboards around the office and updating them regularly with KPIs (sometimes several times per day). The feedback made it easier for teams to experiment with new ideas and make quick decisions about their efficacy.

The pilot was a huge success. Booked sales revenues increased by over 50 percent, and overall customer retention increased by four percent. In terms of some specific behaviours, the number of customer interactions (sales calls) increased by a whopping 72 percent without any increase in headcount, and cash collection increased by 13 percent.

While the financial metrics and efficiency gains were fantastic, what surprised Jeff the most was the dramatic increase in employee engagement. Engagement had been at 13 percent before the program, but after the pilot was completed, that percentage shot up to 87 percent. Jeff realised the real power of the program was not just more efficient work processes, but its ability to change the behaviours of his staff by engaging their seeking systems: self-expression, experimentation, and personalised purpose were all baked into the pilot. With months of practice, the new behaviours became the "frame" within which the team now operated.

Jeff commented that the process "helped leadership get out of the way." Rather than micromanaging performance, and the leaders feeling like they should know all the answers to every issue, the new way of working allowed the whole team to rally around a collective ambition, embrace open communication, and utilise their own unique strengths in order to make progress.

Of course, a pilot across six teams is great, but it doesn't constitute real scale. So, Jeff next planned additional waves of the team journeys in order to cover the organisation's entire "front office." Wave one included 16 teams; wave two, 24. Rather than use external coaches to support the change, this time Jeff used a different approach to transfer the skills from the consultants to local internal coaches, known as "watch one, do one, lead one." First, an internal coach shadowed, or watched, an external consultant as they facilitated a team journey over 12 weeks. Next, they led a team journey with support from external consultants. Finally, they led a team as a fully certified coach without support.

As the work progressed, new teams were asked to volunteer for the next wave of rollout. Providing teams with an opportunity to choose to be involved in the rollout helped raise commitment to the process. For example, one team member named Andrew was one of the worst performing sales managers under the old ways of working. In fact, he had been warned about his low performance several times, and had recently been told that if his performance didn't improve, he would have to be let go. When he heard about the opportunity to be involved in the program, Andrew immediately volunteered his team for the next wave of rollout and became highly involved during the coaching period. Within six weeks, he became the best performing team leader in the company. More broadly, the team rollouts continued being a great success, with overall productivity improvements of 25 to 40 percent. As of 2019, the company had earned an additional £26m of revenue.

Jeff successfully scaled seeking system engagement across his software company by activating his own seeking system, activating the seeking system of small teams, and then capitalising on the success and enthusiasm of those teams to engage others. "At-Scale" usually refers to incorporating a new approach to working into an entire organisation, so that all its employees and teams use it. Leaders often think about scaling using an industrial management lens. This lens is based on scientific management, focusing on making employees adopt standardised and approved processes at the lowest cost – and quickly. The goal of this "rollout approach" is sometimes called "operational scale," and it is achieved by finding efficiencies of standardisation and simplification through replication and cascading.

Since you're reading this book, you already likely know there is a problem with such an approach when trying to scale a new mindset or emotion. If you need to change an organisation fast and often, the industrial lens is limited. In fast-changing environments, you must activate employees' seeking systems so they can help you and the organisation adapt and learn. This new type of change is about scaling *emotional engagement*, and science tells us that our emotions don't scale in the same way as, say, giving employees a new technology to increase production volumes. Transferring *ideas* to other people is different from transferring *emotions*.

Seeking System Cascades Through Contagion

Whenever you try to get someone to understand a new business strategy, use a new technology, or adopt a new sales approach, what you're really trying to do is transfer ideas. Ideas focus on words and logic, which is how most of us think about communication in business. When it comes to creating transformation in an organisation, leaders usually put a lot of emphasis on communicating the right ideas, concepts, and words, typically through speeches, PowerPoint, and documentation. It's a different story when it comes to scaling up the activation of people's seeking systems. Then, it's more important to trigger the right emotions than teach the right ideas. The point is to get people innovating their own ideas and solutions, and experimenting with their own strengths, rather than repeating actions others have decided on.

Words – which are *most* important to understanding ideas – are *least* important in understanding emotions. To activate emotions in others, nonverbal cues are primary,[2] and infection and contagion are essential. Yes, that sounds kind of negative, because those words are usually associated with sickness. But you have surely met someone whose smile was "infectious," right? Just being around them made you smile more. Or think of someone next to you yawning. You likely wanted to yawn when you saw them open their mouth, feeling automatically pulled to do the same.

Contagion refers to how one person's emotions are "caught" by another person. This emotional contagion doesn't happen much at the conscious level; it comes from physiological responses and automatic processes.[3] Emotional contagion is based on uncontrolled, nonverbal cues that emerge during direct interpersonal contact, like facial expression and body language,

27

and on one's tone of voice. So though the sharing of ideas doesn't have to take place face-to-face, the sharing of emotions does. The research shows that this is true whether you look at teams of nurses, accountants, or even professional cricket teams.[4]

For example, in one study, a group of participants was primed to be in a good mood before they gave a leadership speech by being told they had won a five-dollar gift certificate to a local coffee shop.[5] An equal sized group were told "Sorry, you did not win the gift certificate." Leaders in the positive mood condition expressed more positive emotions when giving their leadership speech – who doesn't like free coffee? Perhaps more surprising was the strength of the contagion effect. Audiences who watched the speeches of the leaders who were in a good mood reported more positive emotions themselves – and also performed better in a task they were then given to complete – than those who watched leaders in the negative mood condition. A third audience was in the mix: a group who simply read transcripts of the speeches and did not see them in person. This group experienced no change in mood or performance, showing that the effects on the other two audiences had been due to emotional contagion rather than the content of the speeches.

So how does this work?

The Science of Contagion and Social Influence

Researchers in this area agree that emotional contagion occurs because of individuals' tendency to mimic others' nonverbal behaviour.[6] For example, if a "sender" feels curiosity and enthusiasm because her seeking system is activated, she acts in a way that fits those emotions. Other people in the room – who could be called "targets" – subconsciously mimic those behaviours, cuing them, in turn, to experience the mood they are mimicking. In fact, research shows that just exhibiting a particular facial expression can elicit the corresponding emotion in the target.[7] These mimicry effects, which even occur in infants a few days old, show an innate human tendency toward mimicking others' behaviour.[8]

The bottom line is you can infect the people you are leading or working beside with the positive emotions that come from activating your own seeking system. This infection not only improves your own emotions, it is a leadership tool that increases your ability to scale engagement and increase organisational success: once the sender's positive emotions are "caught" – and the target is infected – the target's performance increases. This improvement takes place for several reasons.

First, positive emotions lead to better decision-making, greater creativity, and being open to more information. Second, positive emotions boost targets' arousal and energy, increasing the effort they put into a task, as well as their persistence on that task. They will have more stamina and resilience because these emotions increase their perceived control and expectations of positive future events. Finally, research shows that positive emotions cause individuals to be more cooperative and helpful – and much more willing to work hard for their leaders.[9]

Leaders can create contagion of positive emotions through excited, authentic smiles because they suggest group cohesion and survival.[10] The opposite is also true – anxious facial displays infect others with negative emotions because they alert other group members about imminent danger (a result of that pesky fear system discussed in Chapter 1).[11]

Even more important to scaling, emotional contagion can reach much further than just "the people in the room." Research shows that positive emotions – and positive behaviours like collaboration and cooperation – cascade throughout social networks. Even people who never personally witnessed a leader's positive emotions, say in a speech, can still be infected by the positive behaviours if they interact with infected audience members who did. One study of cooperative behaviour showed that one group member's positive attitude and behaviour affected other people's future interactions, even though they never saw the initial interaction. Moreover, the study showed how this influence persists across time.[12]

To activate seeking systems at scale, then, you need to start thinking about emotional contagion as a type of *social influence*. Before you ignite employees' seeking systems, you must ignite your own seeking systems. You have to demonstrate – and model – the emotions and behaviours that you want others to "catch." But you can't create scale alone. You need to create or find "carriers," people whose own seeking systems have been activated through the reset, ignite, fuel sequence, who can go out into the organisation and model the emotions and behaviours you hope to create.

You can't just give people a script to memorise and then have them perform speeches in a locked rollout process, either. Carriers must be provided with the latitude to roll out changes using their own strengths and self-expression. They need to be experimenting themselves, curious about how new processes might be invented in each location. They must believe in the purpose of the change in a personal way. To create contagion, your carriers actually need to feel that the rollout is good. Good for the company, yes, but also "a good thing" for its people.

DIGITAL CONTAGION

Emotional contagion can occur over a video screen, which more of us are using than ever before. But you have to work even harder to infect your teams and overall organisation. Video calls require more conscious focus than in-person conversations, so more energy is needed to process non-verbal cues like facial expressions, the tone and pitch of one's voice, and body language.[13] According to Gianpiero Petriglieri, Associate Professor of Organisational Behaviour at INSEAD, video calling creates a situation in which "our minds are together when our bodies feel we're not."[14] He explains, "That dissonance, which causes people to have conflicting feelings, is exhausting." It's still possible to pass along emotional contagion through your phone or computer screen, but it's just harder to initially relax into a conversation naturally. One technique to help improve emotional contagion in video calls is to first rate how expressive you believe you are in face-to-face meetings on a scale of one to ten. Then, whatever the number, try and increase it by 20 percent during your next video call, slightly exaggerating your expressiveness so it comes across clearly.

Five Steps of Scaling

As with the Jeff Lee example at the beginning of this chapter, the reset, ignite, fuel sequence can be repeated at an individual, team, and, finally, an organisational level. The contagion effect shows us, however, that applying these strategies across thousands of people requires a different scaling paradigm than leaders may be used to. It is useful to think about scaling seeking system engagement in terms of running multiple pilots, whether ten, one hundred, or one thousand. Pilots prime teams for the exact attitude needed to engage their seeking systems. They present a challenge with the anticipation of a positive outcome. The teams are typically enthusiastic and keen to experiment with new ideas and processes to help them achieve their goals. And the mindset is focused on learning, where the teams will cycle through their own reset, ignite, and fuel sequence to find an approach that works for them. The approach then uses the principle of emotional contagion to "spread" multiple pilots across the whole enterprise. The rollout should progress in waves, with each new team seeking to "infect" two or three others.

In practice, this new scaling paradigm has been distilled into a series of five steps, which should be kept in mind throughout the remaining chapters:

1. **Activate the seeking system of the top team.** As discussed, activation occurs through the use of the reset, ignite, and fuel sequence (using the strategies, tools, and exercises detailed in the remainder of this book). Start with the top team. Leaders cast a long shadow, and as shown, emotional contagion can be sped up if the leadership teams themselves have fully activated seeking systems. How long this stage takes depends on the nature of the change being proposed. Typically, however, when working with senior teams, this development journey will take around one to three months, during which time the teams cycle through each stage of the reset, ignite, fuel sequence. External facilitators or consultants often assist with this stage.

2. **Identify "carriers" among the top team for the next stage of rollout.** To paraphrase Robert Sutton & Huggy Rao from their book *Scaling Up Excellence*, if you want to spread enthusiasm, you first need some enthusiasm to spread. Leaders whose seeking systems have already been activated through step 1, and have teams of their own, should therefore be the next priority for rollout. At this stage, ask two or three leaders to volunteer to run the process with their teams. Scaling works best when pockets of enthusiasm are first created in small intact teams. Emotional contagion cannot take place unless someone, somewhere, has a fully engaged seeking system. And it cannot spread unless that person "infects" his or her team. From there, the whole team needs to have the opportunity to connect with others to pass the contagion on.

3. **Ensure pilot teams connect and share lessons they've learned.** Up to this stage the rollout may have been under the radar. But as more teams engage with some success, buzz around the organisation will ensue, as

seen in the Bruce Daisley story in Chapter 1. When that happens, it's now time to start sharing those success stories with the rest of the organisation. At this stage, provide mechanisms for the pilot teams to share what they have learned from their own rollout processes. At first, that mechanism may be something as simple as a weekly call for the team leaders. As the rollout progresses, social collaboration platforms or parts of the company intranet may be devoted to success stories and lessons learned. An example of this is the "Welink" platform used by the home health provider Buurtzorg. Small autonomous nursing teams share ideas and post questions on the platform to tap into the collective wisdom of the network. This provides an opportunity to learn from others and innovate locally, continually fuelling the nurses' seeking systems. Whatever mechanism you use for connecting teams, use the platform to invite volunteers for the next stages of the rollout.

4. **Move from cascade to viral.** Since the Covid pandemic, many of us are now familiar with the "R" (or reproduction) number associated with transmissible viruses. R refers to a disease's ability to transmit between people. An R rate of one means an infected person will infect one other person. In the case of a well-run seeking system activation program, you should be looking for an R rate of two to three. That is, each team should be able to "infect" two or three others, who then volunteer for the next wave of the rollout.

    With your leadership team and three teams below them now engaged, the rollout progresses in waves, each typically three times bigger than the previous one. So, wave two may have 15 teams, wave three 45, wave four 135, and so on. This is the point in which the rollout has changed from "cascade" to "viral." The 15 teams in the next wave should not be chosen due to their position in the hierarchy, but because of their passionate enthusiasm for wanting to be involved – they can come from any level of the organisation.

    Practically speaking, the first two waves may have been supported by internal or external consultants, using some of the exercises in this book. Pretty quickly, however, using consultants can often become unsustainable (not to mention unaffordable), so look to employee volunteers from the initial waves to share their experiences and support future waves through further facilitation. Such "train the trainer" models will work here, but only if those being trained have enthusiastically volunteered to facilitate the process.

5. **Designate successful teams as "hubs."** At this point, you will be able to start creating a critical mass of "champions," carriers of positive emotions whose seeking systems are engaged as they help other teams. At a team level it's possible to designate the teams made up of these champions as "hubs." In a global organisation you may have one hub per geographic region. These hubs then replicate steps one through four in their own areas.

The Five Steps in Practice

To see these five steps in practice, let's consider an investment management company's attempt to roll out a new organisational purpose. This example shows an emotional transformation – one that required a new mindset to realise its benefits – and was therefore ideal for the emotion contagion scaling paradigm. As with many organisations, this firm wanted their purpose statement to reflect their role in society and speak to multiple stakeholders. They hoped the statement would be meaningful for employees and customers and signal that the company stood for something bigger than profit. They also knew that a powerful purpose could unleash the enthusiasm of its employees, but only if the employees emotionally connected with it. The hard part – and the real test of any organisation's purpose – was figuring out how to make the purpose more than just words on a poster.

For the first step – activating the seeking system of the top team – the company's top team spent a week at an off-site retreat, reflecting, exploring their role in society, considering their own legacy, and experimenting with different purpose statements that inspired them. They decided on "bringing financial wellbeing to all our stakeholders." Since they had created the new statement together, leadership felt vested in the purpose. With their own seeking systems engaged, it was time to get others in the organisation excited about the new purpose.

While it would have been tempting – and common practice – to start communicating the purpose in town halls and leadership speeches, the leadership team decided instead to take employees through a purpose activation journey (discussed in Chapter 7) and to use the principles of emotional contagion to scale to all employees. So, in step two – identify "carriers" among the top team – three highly enthused leaders from the senior team volunteered to pilot the purpose activation approach in their own teams.

33

The approach involved deepening employee understanding of the organi-sational purpose while also exploring employees' strengths and motivations. These three carriers encouraged their team members to find ways of using their strengths in service of their own motivations and the organisational purpose. A group of consultants facilitated the carriers and teams' discus-sions, which lasted a few weeks. (Notice how these first two steps in the process resemble a typical hierarchical "cascade," with the important caveat that only enthusiastic leaders who volunteer are involved in the next round of the rollout.)

In step three – connecting the pilot teams to share the lessons they've learned – the three pilot teams ran an "After Action Review" process (explored in Chapter 5) to reflect on what they learned and were encour-aged to talk to the rest of the business about their experiences. A low-level buzz started to emerge, and a call was put out for volunteers for the next round of rollout. Leaders at any level were invited to volunteer their teams, and those that had interacted with the pilot teams were keen to do so.

Next up, step four: from cascade to viral. Nine diverse teams were chosen for the next wave based on the volunteer requests, not based on their posi-tion in the hierarchy. This choice helped to build momentum with frontline teams, who often have the most to gain from greater seeking system activa-tion. Experienced consultants facilitated all these sessions. Employees felt guided on a personal journey to help them use their strengths in service of the new organisational purpose. They reported being "infected by the enthu-siasm in the room" in these early sessions.

The next wave included up to 30 teams (based on the principle that each team "infects" at least two to three others). At this point, the firm had a decision to make: Do they continue the rollout with consulting support, or find a more cost-effective option? Alternative options were discussed, including certifying internal trainers and creating a workbook of self-guided exercises that individuals could use at their own pace. What happened next was instructional in itself. Adopting the workbook option for the next wave, the program started to lose momentum. Remember, emotional contagion works through non-verbal cues from other infected people – not through reading a workbook.

The people who roll out a new program are just as important as the meth-odology they are rolling out. Simply identifying a project team and provid-ing them with an instruction manual will not cut it, even though the steps listed may be the same. People who had succeeded in the pilot locations should have been allowed to help the people in the following wave to both implement change and adapt the sequence to local needs and constraints. As mentioned, seeking system engagement is only contagious from others who also have their own seeking systems engaged. That engagement is best achieved when all the triggers are deliberately built into a program of work, using the reset, ignite, fuel sequence.

Step five is about creating hubs, successful teams of "champions." When you activate employees' seeking systems and great results ensue, you will become noticeable and attractive to other parts of the organisation. As engagement grows, the result will be a centre of excellence, featuring excited employees in a vibrant, fast, creative workplace, with business results that stand out. The investment management company employees who had been involved in the early waves did become beacons of emotional engagement and were able to support and infect others, though that support could have been more effective without the later implementation of the workbook approach. Still, they continued to share lessons and tell stories of how they had activated and personalised the organisational purpose. Their infectious enthusiasm and ability to personalise the organisational purpose inspired others to reframe how they thought about the purpose and experiment with ways to bring it to life for themselves.

Summary

- Seeking system activation is an emotional transformation, and emotions scale differently than ideas. Rather than scaling through an industrial cascade of communications, aim to employ the emotional contagion effect, where teams of highly engaged employees "infect" others.
- Seeking system engagement is only contagious from others who also have their own seeking systems engaged; that engagement is best achieved when all the triggers are deliberately built into a program of work, using the reset, ignite, fuel sequence.
- Seeking system activation is best done in small teams or work units, using the mindset of a "pilot" implementation throughout. Each team can then tailor the approach to their particular needs, experiment, learn, and see the impact on their own work unit – integrating all the seeking system triggers.
- There are five main steps to scaling seeking system activation within an organisation, which build on the principle of emotional contagion.

Starting with the top team, subsequent teams are chosen based on their enthusiasm to participate, not on what may be logistically effective, and not on a hierarchical cascade.

- As rollout happens best in intact teams, the strategies and exercises in the rest of this book are focused on activities that will help teams to reset, ignite, and fuel their seeking systems.

Notes

1   Milkman, Katy (2021) *How to Change: The Science of Getting from Where You Are to Where You Want to Be*. London, England: Penguin.

2   Barsade, S.G. (2002) "The ripple effect: emotional contagion and its influence on group behavior." *Administrative Science Quarterly* 47: 644–667; Mehrabian, A. (1972) *Nonverbal Communication*. Chicago, IL: Aldine-Atherton.

3   Neumann, R., and F. Strack (2000) "Mood contagion: the automatic transfer of mood between persons." *Journal of Personality and Social Psychology* 79: 211–223.

4   Totterdell, P. (2000) "Catching moods and hitting runs: mood linkage and subjective performance in professional sport teams." *Journal of Applied Psychology* 85: 848–859; Totterdell, P., S. Kellet, K. Teuchmann, and R.B. Briner (1998) "Evidence of mood linkage in work groups." *Journal of Personality and Social Psychology* 74: 1504–1515.

5   Johnson, S.K. (2009) "Do you feel what I feel? Mood contagion and leadership outcomes." *The Leadership Quarterly* 20: 814–827.

6   Hatfield, E.J., C.K. Hsee, J. Costello, and M.S. Weisman (1995) "The impact of vocal feedback on emotional experience and expression." *Journal of Social Behavior and Personality* 10: 293–312.

7   Chartrand, T.L., and J.A. Bargh (1999) "The chameleon effect: the perception-behavior link and social interaction." *Journal of Personality and Social Psychology* 76: 893–910; Adelman, P.K., and R. Zajonc (1989) "Facial efference and the experience of emotion." *Annual Review of Psychology* 40: 249–280.

8   Wild, B., M. Erb, and M. Bartels (2001) "Are emotions contagious? Evoked emotions while viewing emotionally expressive faces: quality, quantity, time course and gender differences." *Psychiatry Research* 102: 109–124.

9   Barsade, S.G. (2002) "The ripple effect: emotional contagion and its influence on group behavior." *Administrative Science Quarterly* 47: 644–667.

10 Jehn, K.A. (1995) "A multimethod examination of the benefits and detriments of intragroup conflict." *Administrative Science Quarterly* 40: 256–282; Carver,

C.S., A. Kus, and M.F. Scheier (1994) "Effects of good versus bad mood and optimistic versus pessimistic outlook on social acceptance versus rejection." *Journal of Social and Clinical Psychology* 13: 138–151.

11 Levenson, R.W. (1996) "Biological substrates of empathy and facial modulation of emotion: two facets of the scientific legacy of John Lanzetta." *Motivation and Emotion* 20: 185–204.

12 Fowler, James H., and Nicholas A. Christakis (2010) "Cooperative behavior cascades in human social networks." *PNAS* 107, no. 12: 5334–5338. https://doi.org/10.1073/pnas.0913149107

13 Jiang, M. (2020) *The Reason Zoom Calls Drain Your Energy.* www.bbc.com/worklife/article/20200421-why-zoom-video-chats-are-soexhausting

14 Ibid.

PART 2   **Reset**

3 | Making Space

In March of 2020, the COVID-19 pandemic threw many businesses into full-blown crisis management mode. Organisations grappled with financial and liquidity issues. Navigating complicated government support programs and overcoming supply chain challenges, they had to find new ways to serve their customers and develop new business strategies, all while protecting their brand. Their leaders faced enormous challenges managing their workforce – furloughing workers, working from home, establishing safe working practices, managing employee safety and well-being, and planning for a new way of work post-COVID. Confronted with such complexity, many businesses treated the pandemic as an opportunity to reset.

Such seismic shifts in an environment act as a jolt for individuals and organisations, shaking them out of established routines and providing an opportunity to take different approaches. As part of his "Great Reset" agenda, Klauss Schwab, Founder and Executive Chairman of the World Economic Forum, says "The pandemic represents a rare but narrow window of opportunity to reflect, re-imagine, and reset our world."[1] With the unimaginable devastation the pandemic has caused, leaders are looking for a silver lining on the horizon, attempting to rescue the blessing from the curse.

To reset, no matter the circumstances, we need to reach a mental state called *focused curiosity*. This state is one in which we have first reduced our cognitive load – enabling us to focus on what matters – and then regulated our emotional state, reducing any anxious, defensive, or judgmental feelings that could negatively impact the quality of our thinking. The most useful emotional state for a reset is one of genuine curiosity, a mindset that can intentionally create wonder, intrigue, and anticipation out of almost any situation. Focused curiosity allows us to let go of the past, make space

DOI: 10.4324/9781003396833-6

for ourselves, and put our minds at ease. It's nearly impossible to ignite the seeking system while our brains are overstimulated and we feel emotionally anxious; this was true before the pandemic, just as it is true now.

When we become over-stimulated, too much electrical activity takes place in our pre-frontal cortex – the site of all our cognition – using up valuable working memory. Overwhelm can also lead to anxiety or panic, sometimes called an "amygdala hijack." When our prefrontal cortex gets overloaded, this can trigger a high anxiety response in the amygdala, potentially crippling performance. Low performance leads to further negative feelings as we spend all our time worrying about how much we have to do, rather than doing any of it. Since quality of thinking is linked to mood, and vice versa, clear-headed thinking and a positive emotional state can lead to an upward spiral of performance, while cognitive overload and a negative emotional state can lead to a downward one.

To reduce cognitive load, we need to reduce the *demand* on our working memories, and to regulate our emotions, we need to calm the amygdala by directing our energy toward curiosity. In the process, a reset occurs, and we set the stage for both igniting and fuelling our seeking systems. Of course, we want the benefits of focused curiosity to extend to our team members and overall organisation as well.

The real question is: How can we achieve an effective reset that will directly enhance the well-being of employees? Easier read than done, of course, but there are valid strategies that can help. As shown in Figure 3.1,

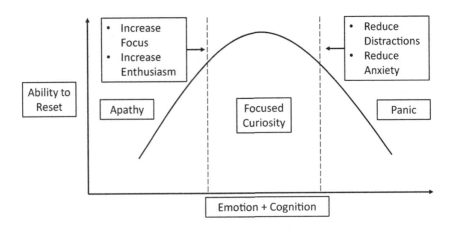

Figure 3.1

Ability to Reset

to obtain just the right amount of focus you can either employ strategies that *reduce* distractions or strategies that *increase* focus. Likewise, to obtain just the right emotional state you can either *reduce* anxiety, and similar negative emotions, or *increase* enthusiasm, and similar positive emotions.

The main focus of this chapter is to look at systemic changes that leaders can make to their organisations that will allow employees to regularly reset. As we now know, however, for a leader to ignite the seeking system in others they must first ignite their own. What follows, therefore, are some simple *individual* strategies for effecting a reset that my clients and I have found useful.

The objective of using these strategies is to reach a state of focused curiosity. This means that if you are languishing or feeling apathetic, employ strategies to increase your focus (cognition) and enthusiasm (emotion). If you are feeling overwhelmed or panicked, the place to start is by reducing distractions (cognition) and your anxiety (emotion). This is not an exhaustive list, and the tools will require experimentation to figure out which ones work for you:

Category	Strategy	Steps
Reduce Distractions	1. De-clutter	Reduce cognitive load by de-cluttering the following: a. **Working memory**. Get things out of your head by immediately writing things down as they occur to you, or by having a recording device with you at all times. b. **Physical space**. Tidy your desk, switch off e-mail, put your phone on airplane mode, work in a place where you have worked well in the past. c. **Decisions**. Decision making is one of the most energy-intensive functions of our prefrontal cortex. Avoid extraneous decision making by making easy decisions automatic so you can conserve valuable cognitive energies for the decisions that matter. Albert Einstein famously didn't bother remembering his phone number. Mark Zuckerberg has said he owns 20 identical grey T-shirts so he doesn't have to worry about what to wear every day.

(Continued)

(Continued)

Category	Strategy	Steps
	2. Learn to say "no"	Adam Grant, the Saul P. Steinberg professor of management and professor of psychology at Wharton, has written about strategies for saying no without offending people. These are my favourites: a. **Create policies.** When you say no by referring to your policy, it removes the feeling of personal rebuttal. "I have a policy of never working in my protected time" feels much better than "I don't have time for that right now." b. **Use a relational account.** This involves referencing your commitment to other people when declining a request. "My top priority is to deliver this client request on time. If I helped you, I would be letting them down." c. **Deflect.** Helpful ways of deflecting requests include making referrals ("this isn't my thing, but I know someone who may be able to help"); connecting people with similar requests ("you are both working on similar things, you should connect); or deferrals ("I'm swamped at the moment but do follow up again").
	3. Simplify Information	Three techniques that can help to simplify information and so reduce cognitive load: a. **Chunking**: Group the long lists of tasks, problems, and activities you need to focus on in any given day into a maximum of four key areas of focus. b. **Visualisation**: Use graphs, tables, and mind-maps to illustrate key concepts. Metaphor and storytelling also help to create visual imagery that simplifies complex concepts. c. **Salience**: Try to reduce complex concepts into one or two core ideas that describe the essence of the situation. Try the creative pitch technique known as "high concept:" the movie *Alien* was famously pitched as "Jaws in space."
Increase Focus	1. Prioritise Prioritisation	Prioritisation is one of the brain's most energy-sapping processes. Start every week by prioritising your most important, non-urgent, tasks for that week. These are the 3–4 strategic tasks that will make the biggest difference to your long term performance. Schedule blocks of time to work on these priorities.

Category	Strategy	Steps
	2. Time-block Deep Work	Once you schedule your important tasks, make your focus laser sharp by following these steps: a. **Run a pre-focus ritual**. Tidy your individual workspace, switch off your cell phone, and disable e-mail alerts. Next, put a glass of water on your desk, sit quietly in your seat, and focus on your breathing for one minute. Then set a timer for 90 minutes. When done regularly, such intentional repetition has been shown to regulate performance, helping people to act in a steadier, more focused way. b. **Work uninterrupted on one important, non-urgent task for 90 minutes**. There is some evidence to show that the cycling of various biological processes throughout the day – called ultradian rhythms – can affect our concentration. The optimum amount of time to focus appears to be around 90 minutes. c. **Stop working once the alarm goes off, then celebrate completion of the exercise with a 20-minute reset break**. Give yourself 20 minutes to take a short walk, go outside, or call a loved one. Dr. Ernest Rossi, a US psychotherapist who studies ultradian rhythms, recommends a 20-minute break after intense focused activity. The anticipation of a small reward – in this case, a restorative break – is also enough to reduce amygdala activity and boost the release of dopamine.
	3. Focused Curiosity Meditation	Create immediate focus via a short meditation. Focusing attention on your breath or bodily sensations activates brain regions involved in perceiving information coming into the senses. This has the effect of deactivating the pre-frontal cortex which reduces cognitive load, clears the mind, and creates focus.
Reduce Anxiety	1. Create Psychological Distance	Ethan Kross, professor of psychology and management/organisations at the University of Michigan, specialises in emotion regulation. He has written about strategies to harness the "inner voice" in your head through gaining psychological distance.

(Continued)

(Continued)

Category	Strategy	Steps
		Psychological distance is the degree to which people feel removed from a phenomenon, and the greater the distance, the greater the reduction in amygdala activity. Distance in this case is not limited to the physical surroundings, but can include social distancing, temporal distancing, spatial distancing, and cognitive distancing. Here are a few of my favourite strategies: a. **Distanced Self Talk** – use your name and the second person "you" to refer to yourself (creates social distance). b. **Imagine advising a friend** – think about what advice you would give to a friend experiencing the same problem as you (creates social distance). c. **Mental time travel** – think about how you will feel in a year (creates temporal distance). d. **Fly on the wall** – visualise the situation from the perspective of a fly peering down on the event (creates spatial distance). e. **Reframe your experience as a challenge** – reinterpret the situation not as a threat, but as a challenge you can handle (creates cognitive distance).
	2. Emotion Re-appraisal	Anxiety and excitement are often referred to by psychologists as "high arousal" states, and their physiological effects are very similar: sweaty palms, raised heart rate, dilated pupils, etc. Studies by Alison Wood-Brooks have shown that re-appraising anxiety as excitement can lead to significantly improved performance. So, next time you think you may be feeling anxious, notice how your body is reacting and say out loud "I must be feeling excited."
	3. Affect Labelling	Label a negative emotion as soon as you experience it. This re-directs your brain function to the prefrontal cortex, dampening the chances of an amygdala hijack. It is important to do this as soon as you experience the negative emotion, otherwise it can take hold and it takes much more mental effort to stop (depleting resources in the prefrontal cortex).

Category	Strategy	Steps
Increase Enthusiasm	1. Create Awe	As we tap into something vast, complex, or meaningful, our sense of self shrinks. At the same time, our desire to connect with and help others increases. People who experience awe also report higher levels of overall life satisfaction and well-being.
		Two useful strategies to seek out awe in your daily life are to zoom out and zoom in. Both require developing a deep curiosity about the world around us.
		a. **Zoom out**. Reflect on something vast, such as the night sky, nearby mountains, or the height of skyscrapers dotting the skyline. b. **Zoom in** on something tiny, appreciating the wonder of the patterns of wood grain on your kitchen table, or the shapes of the leaves on the trees outside.
	2. Focus on Your Strengths	A powerful way of increasing people's enthusiasm is to focus on their strengths. Using your strengths to make a positive influence on others creates real satisfaction in your work and life.
	3. Keep a Gratitude Journal	Martin Speligmen, one of the fathers of positive psychology, has pioneered many strategies for increasing happiness. One of the best known and effective is to keep a gratitude journal. Write three things you are grateful for in a journal every evening for two weeks. In addition, provide a causal explanation for each good thing.

Having managed an individual reset, let's take a look at each of these categories again and think about what systemic changes can be made to enable a reset at scale. The tools and approaches explored can help your teams and overall organisation get into a state of focused curiosity, reset, and activate their seeking systems.

Reduce Distractions

Humans have evolved such that we are always open to new data. Whether it represents a threat or an opportunity, this information causes us to become distracted. Since that's the case, one of the most effective strategies to help us focus our attention on what is most important is to *reduce* the data coming in from the outside world. To reduce distractions at a team or organisational level, we must first *simplify*.

Simplify

Complexity overwhelms our prefrontal cortex, causing us to spend our best cognitive hours figuring out how to navigate bureaucratic systems, instead of focusing on activities that are both fulfilling and value adding for the business. To simplify and lighten our cognitive load, then, we must "subtract." Abstract painter Hans Hoffmann may have described it best: "The ability to simplify means to eliminate the unnecessary, so that the necessary may speak."[2] This art of allowing the necessary to "speak" can be approached in four distinct steps:

1. **Frame the simplicity challenge.** Identify areas of complexity and frame the challenge using positive language that prompts a focus on what will be gained from the challenge, not on what might be lost.
2. **Map the system or process**. Understand the essence of the complex system or process and what it is trying to achieve.
3. **Create simple rules that describe the essence**. Create rules to help *remove* steps from the system or process, as compared to adding or changing them. Describe the new process as a simple "rule of thumb" to help achieve the essence.
4. **Experiment and measure the impact**. Test the newly simplified system or process and measure the impact.

As a simple example of these steps in practice, consider Tobi Lütke, founder and CEO of Shopify, the multi-billion-dollar e-commerce company. Lütke – like knowledge workers the world over – was getting increasingly frustrated at the time he and his teams spent in meetings. According to Steven Rogelberg of UNC Charlotte, who wrote *The Surprising Science of Meetings*, pre-Covid-19 studies showed that about 55 million meetings a day were held in the US alone,[3] and due to how unproductive they were, a whopping $37 billion was wasted on them annually.[4] Many people at Shopify joked that they spent eight hours a day in meetings and only then were they able to get on with their "real" work. The practice seemed ripe for overload, burnout, and wasted money and resources, so Lütke decided something must be done. Though all of the details of his process were not published, like most successful simplicity efforts I've observed, it broadly followed the four steps as outlined below.

Step One: Frame the Simplicity Challenge

Lütke conducted an analysis with his employees and found that about half of all meetings at Shopify were not viewed as valuable. He asked, "How do we create more time to focus on the activities that matter to us?" This framed the challenge around the potential gain, as compared to "How do we reduce the number of meetings we have?" This would have been framed around a potential loss. The focus was on saving time. Time was chosen as the key KPI because it is simple, tangible, and universal; it also translates well to reducing activity.

Step Two: Map the System or Process

Lütke asked what most meetings were trying to achieve, and considered both stated meeting objectives and unspoken benefits, like the opportunity for teams to connect. Meetings were part of a wider organisational system designed to effectively deliver an exceptional e-commerce experience. The main question – the essence of the company's meeting culture – was whether or not these meetings helped to deliver this exceptional customer experience. Lütke thought not.

Step Three: Create Simple Rules That Describe the Essence

As a software engineer, Lütke knows the importance of building resilience into his technical architecture. He regularly switches off servers just to test whether the Shopify site can keep running, and he sometimes asks his employees to work with their computer mouse in their non-dominant hand for a day to check how difficult operating the site has become. He decided to apply the same principles to the practice of holding meetings in his company. So, to see how the business would cope, Lütke cancelled them – all of them. The rule of thumb seemed to become "if in doubt, avoid meetings." A somewhat extreme position, possibly, but it certainly provided an emotional jolt.

Step Four: Experiment and Measure Impact

Many people within the company found it difficult to let go of all meetings, so after a brief experiment they have since arranged a system to hold them, but only when they are deemed to actually help deliver an exceptional e-commerce experience.[5] Repeating meetings on the same topics, however, is not allowed.

By radically cutting the number of meetings, Lütke reduced cognitive load across the company, finding more time to focus on the work that really mattered for Shopify's customers. Whatever the target of your simplicity efforts, the process can help your whole workforce reduce unnecessary distractions, creating a company-wide reset.

Prioritise

Aside from simplifying, there is no better way to reduce distractions than through prioritisation. Without effective prioritisation, nothing important will receive the attention it deserves. Prioritisation not only limits distractions and focuses attention but can also act as an important motivational tool by allowing teams to visualise the steps they must take to achieve their goal. The problem with prioritising is that the very activity takes a lot of cognitive energy, so do your prioritising when your team is fresh. Make use of temporal landmarks and do your prioritising first thing on a Monday morning, say, before the busyness of the week sets in.

Whichever tools you use to prioritise – and even a cursory look at productivity literature reveals there are many – the important thing to do is to make prioritisation and de-prioritisation part of your weekly working practice. Here are two simple team-based exercises that can be used to help prioritise activities to ensure a focus on what matters most.

Exercise: The $100 Test

What Is It?

The $100 test assigns relative value to a list of activities you must perform, or problems you must solve, by allocating an imaginary $100 across them. By using the concept of cash, the exercise makes salient the impact of your prioritisation on business value and acts a proxy for the effort that should be expended on each item. The exercise also gives you the opportunity to consider, and at times reconsider, your reasons for the particular allocation. The test can be applied in any context and works well as part of a group discussion to help to align priorities across a team.

How Long Does It Take?

Thirty minutes to two hours, depending on the length of the list and size of the group.

Group Size?

Up to 10 people.

How Does It Work?

Step One

Gather your team together and agree on a list of items to be prioritised. This list may be of improvement projects for the year, potential features on a new product, or simply the activities the team has identified as necessary to meet their objectives.

Step Two

Create a blank table on a flipchart, or similar visual aid, using the headings shown in Table 3.1. Explain the challenge of having a collective $100 to spend on the list of items, with the amount allocated representing the importance of the items. In a list of three items, for example, one may receive $20, another may receive $65, and the third, $15. Give the group sufficient time to discuss and assign their values, then ask them to write an explanation for the amounts allocated. In the example shown in Table 3.1, the test is applied to a set of activities for increasing sales revenues.

Make sure no one gets hung up on focusing on the literal cost of items on the list; have them focus instead on their relative value or importance to the team and overall organisation.

Step Three

Discuss the group's decisions and reasoning. If the money has been equally spread out, try forcing greater prioritisation by only allowing a minimum

Table 3.1 $100 Test

Topic/Item/Issue	$	Why?
Cross selling to existing clients	30	Much easier to expand work with existing clients who trust us.
Lowering margin to increase sales	10	Required to be competitive but could be brand damaging and difficult to recover margins.
Speaking at conferences	5	Good brand building but less targeted.
Publishing "thought leader-ship" papers	5	Good brand building but less targeted.
Holding webinars/round table discussions	15	More intimate and targeted at new/existing clients.
Social media campaigns	5	Good brand building but less targeted.
Linking payment for performance	10	A mechanism of de-risking a purchase for the client. Builds trust in our ability to deliver by having "skin in the game."
Start small and build – sell a small piece of work and grow it	20	De-risks a purchase for the client and pro-vides an opportunity to build trust. Difficult to be profitable unless we sell on.

Source: The source of the $100 test is unknown.

allocation of $25, meaning some items will need to receive $0. Or ask the group to compare two items of the same value. If they had to choose one, which would it be? Next, ask how the allocation should relate to the actual resources you have available. For example, a $5 allocation translates to 5 percent of your available team resources. Agree how the allocation will translate to the work that now has to be done.

Impact/Effort Matrix

What Is It?

In this decision-making exercise, possible actions are mapped on a matrix, shown in Figure 3.2, based on two factors: the effort (or cost) required to implement the action and the potential impact (or value) of the action.

As shown, high impact, high effort actions may include big bets, such as a major IT investment, transformation program, or acquisition of another company. Quick wins may fall under high impact, low effort, and dreaded money pits would be listed in the high effort, low impact quadrant. Then

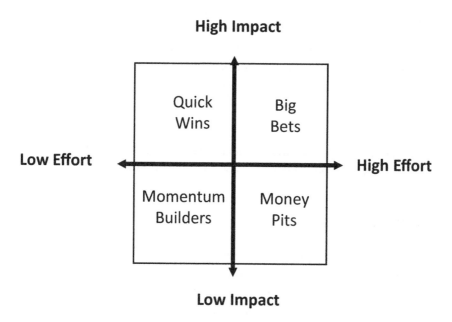

Figure 3.2 Impact/Effort Matrix

Source: the original source of the impact/effort matrix is unknown

there are the low impact, low effort actions, often called momentum build-ers, as they only use minimum time and resources, but still show positive progress toward the goal, even if the impact is small.

How Long Does It Take?

Thirty minutes to two hours, depending on the number of items being con-sidered and the size of the group.

Group Size?

Up to 10 people.

How Does It Work?

Step One

Gather your team, print out a version of the matrix, or draw one on the eraser board, and ask: "What needs to be done to achieve our strategic goal?"

Step Two

Have team members write responses on a series of sticky notes. Discuss each one with the team to decide where the responses would fall on the matrix, then place the notes accordingly.

Step Three

As a group, discuss the relative impact or effort that will help to balance and evaluate the suggested actions before committing to them.

Increase Focus

When it comes to improving our cognition, in addition to removing distractions we can aim to increase our focus. People often say our brains are like muscles – to get stronger, they need training. That is certainly true of our ability to increase our focus. Research by the late Clifford Nass of Stanford showed that too much unfocused time degrades our ability to focus when we need to.[6] So, finding opportunities to practice focused attention is a critical first step in increasing our focus and to do this you need to normalise focus time.

Normalise Focus Time

Focus provides the ability to work distraction-free on important tasks for a defined period. To do so at scale, it needs to become culturally acceptable for knowledge workers to schedule and protect focus time, and they should receive guidance on how best to use it. There are a number of steps leaders should follow to support employees in incorporating focus time into their everyday activities.

Step One: Promote Focus Time

Leaders should encourage every member of their team to schedule focus time at the start of each week. If you try to schedule focus time at the start of every day, employees will likely struggle to set aside what is already *urgent*. When done at the start of each week, however, it is much easier to optimise for what is *important*, and schedule and protect that time accordingly. For most knowledge workers, the goal should be one to four hours of focus time per day.

Responding to overwhelm during the pandemic, KFC in the UK, with over 1,000 restaurants and 30,000 staff members, instructed all head staff to book 60 minutes each day for focus time, marked as "leave me the cluck alone" in their shared calendars. With the whole team working from home during lockdown, the company went further to signal the importance of protecting time by blocking out "virtual commute time" in everybody's schedules. No calls or meetings were allowed between 8 and 9 am or between 5:30 and 6:30 pm. Providing employees with this dedicated focus time emphasised the need to address what was most important throughout the week and gave them some well-deserved down time too.

Step Two: Provide Guidance

Once employees have scheduled important tasks, many benefit from guidance on how best to use that time. While every individual will have a different approach that best suits them, science gives us some pointers. Ask your employees to try the following during a dedicated two-hour focus period:

- **Run a pre-focus ritual.** Tidy your individual workspace, switch off your cell phone, and disable e-mail alerts. Next, put a glass of water on your desk, sit quietly in your seat, and focus on your breathing for one minute. Then set a timer for 90 minutes. When done regularly, such intentional repetition has been shown to regulate performance, helping people to act in a steadier, more focused way. Inclusion of the breathing exercise activates our brains' regions involved in perceiving information coming into the senses. This has the effect of deactivating the pre-frontal cortex, reducing cognitive load, and allowing us to focus.
- **Work uninterrupted on one important, non-urgent task for 90 minutes.** There is evidence to show that the cycling of various biological processes throughout the day – called ultradian rhythms – can affect our concentration. The optimum amount of time to focus appears to be around 90 minutes.[7]
- **Stop working once the alarm goes off, then celebrate completion of the exercise with a 20-minute reset break.** Give yourself 20 minutes to take a short walk, go outside, or call a loved one. Dr Ernest Rossi, a US psychotherapist who studies ultradian rhythms, recommends a 20-minute break after intense focused activity. The anticipation of a small reward – in this case, a restorative break – is also enough to reduce amygdala activity and boost the release of dopamine.[8]

Step Three: Keep Going

In order to normalise focus time, it must become a habit, which requires repetition and practice. Leaders should role-model the use of protected focus time to give their team members the permission to do the same. Maintaining the schedules employees set for their important, uninterrupted work is difficult, as it often feels easier and more efficient to tick off tasks that demand an immediate, specific response, compared to working on something important but open-ended.

One way to increase participation in focus time is to introduce the 1–2 combination of "streaks and exceptions." Achieving a "streak" of daily focus time sessions gamifies the approach and can lead to greater participation as people strive to maintain their streak. Then encourage people to allow themselves one exception per week to miss a focus time session if their will power waivers or life just gets in the way. Research shows that making explicit allowances for the odd exception keeps our self-confidence and desire to continue intact. We discuss this and other habit building techniques in more detail in Chapter 9.

In a 2020 study, Dan Cable and Laura Giurge from London Business School designed a "focus time" intervention that broadly followed these three steps.[9] In the study, employees engaged in a 30-minute weekly planning session at the start of each week and were instructed to make a list of their important, non-urgent tasks. They ranked the tasks' level of importance relative to each other, and blocked two hours per day in their calendars for the remaining four days to work on the most important tasks that were not urgent. Employees were instructed to work on only one important, non-urgent work task during each two-hour period. They were further instructed to turn off or remove, as much as possible, any digitals tools that could distract them during that time. Results from the six-week field experiment showed that employees who engaged in this focus time experienced lower burnout and expressed more positive beliefs about their work contributions.

> **THE PROBLEM WITH FEAR**
>
> An important note on fear: as most leaders instinctively know, fear is highly effective in helping people to increase their focus. By bringing "urgency" to a task and highlighting the consequenc-

es of failure, a leader's team members are likely to take note and focus in on that task. At a neurological level, fear releases norepinephrine, which brings a deep and immediate alertness. This tunnel vision remains in place until the given threat recedes. Fear is therefore effective in the short term if we want people to do more of what they already know how to do. However, as we discussed earlier in the book, too much fear reduces dopamine and makes it almost impossible to ignite the seeking system, so avoid using fear as a tool to increase focus. When people do feel overly anxious, you need to take steps to reduce it.

Reduce Anxiety

Psychological safety, a term popularised by Harvard Business School Professor Amy Edmundson,[10] is a belief that we will not be punished or humiliated for speaking up with our ideas, questions, or concerns, or for making mistakes. We feel psychologically safe when activity in the amygdala is reduced in a social setting, a result of reducing our threat response. When applied to leading employees in their reset, psychological safety often boils down to some key leadership behaviours which deliver targeted signals at key points that cue safety and belonging in employees. These signals include showing vulnerability ("I may be wrong here . . ."), actively inviting input from others ("I value your input; what do you think we should do?"), treating all feedback as a gift ("Thank you for raising that, let's discuss what we can learn . . ."), showing gratitude ("I really appreciate what you did here . . ."), and, of course, demonstrating focused curiosity ("Tell me more about that . . .").

Delivering the right signal at the right time takes an understanding of your individual team members – and plenty of trial and error. While there is no perfect formula for this process, there is a simple framework that can be useful in prompting leaders to demonstrate these behaviours to build psychological safety. Enter the 3C's.

3C's Framework: Consult, Consider, Close

The 3C's framework was developed by Michael Parke, an assistant professor of management at The Wharton School, and is designed to increase psychological safety and encourage employee voice. The framework consists of three components: consult, consider, and close.

- **Consult**: Explicitly invite people to provide feedback and voice ideas, suggestions, and concerns. Asking for feedback shows your own vulnerability, while also signaling you care about what your employees have to say and that you will consider action based on their input. As an example, if you plan to hold a brainstorming meeting with your team to discuss new product ideas, tell attendees in advance that you'll be looking for everyone to provide ideas, however tentative. This heads up gives introverts time to prepare and gets everyone started out on the same page. In the meeting, you might ask for everyone's ideas before putting forward any of your own, signaling you really are interested in the team's input.
- **Consider**: People understand that not every idea they bring to the table will be implemented, but they want to know their voice was heard, so always show appreciation when people suggest ideas or provide feedback. Asking people for their ideas and then ignoring them can seriously backfire, so you need to prove you've considered what they've said.[11]
- **Close**: Follow up to let people know what happened to their ideas. You can even make this a routine event, which is also a good way to hold yourself, and other leaders, accountable for providing feedback (research shows that holding leaders accountable also increases psychological safety across the group).[12]

In one study with a healthcare organisation, Parke and his colleagues showed how easy it can be to scale the implementation of the 3C's framework and institutionalise the approach across an enterprise. The company provided concierge services for doctors and was considering eight initiatives that they thought would improve the doctors' experience. In the control group, the doctors were sent details of the initiatives via a simple e-mail communication and promised updates which were sent every two weeks. The "consult only" group was told about the initiatives and then also asked for their opinions about them. The "consult/consider/close" group was told about the initiative, asked for their opinions (consult), given a summary of the feedback received (consider), and informed of any decisions taken as a result (close).

Following the four-month period of two weekly e-mail communications to half of the company, all participating doctors were asked about their desire to participate in the changes at the company and also about the company's perceived impact. The 3C's condition provided the strongest effect, with a 10 percent increase in participation and an 18 percent increase in perceived impact, compared with the control group.

Increase Enthusiasm

As well as *reducing* the threat response, it's also possible to *increase* the quality of our emotional state by sparking interest and enthusiasm. American psychologist Martin Seligman, often referred to as the father of positive psychology, showed how positive emotions help us tap into our brains' potential by improving our mental functioning. Positive emotions open us up to new information and ways of thinking, improve our creativity, and help us make better decisions.

We can feel these uplifts of enthusiasm when we have an experience that rises above the routine and sparks joy, gratitude, or amazement. We can all identify moments in our personal or professional lives that lifted us in this way: an amazing vacation, a team celebration, an instance when people rallied round us in a time of need, an unexpected "thank you" from the boss. These experiences need not happen by accident – they can be designed. As a leader, it's important to identify and attend to these moments.

Attend to the Moments That Matter

We all experience moments where we are searching for a feeling. Unsure, vulnerable, or just curious, these are the moments where we look for cues that tell us how to feel – either positive or negative – which will impact our subsequent decisions and behaviour. These are the circumstances that demand attention, and it is the job of leaders to be positive in these moments that matter.

Imagine you work in one of the biggest professional services firms in the world. Known for technical excellence and unrivalled service, surveys consistently place you in the top five most prestigious consulting brands. Popular with clients and candidates alike, you receive approximately 200 quality applicants for every advertised vacancy. You have a "best in class" recruitment process that includes verbal and numerical reasoning tests, observed group exercises, and 1:1 competency-based interviews. You always look for the best of the best to join your team.

So imagine how disappointed you would feel if, after an enormous effort to find the right candidates, around 50 percent of applicants who were offered a position subsequently turned it down? Many of these candidates have choices, of course. They may be interviewing with a number of prospective employers, and they are of course talented, worthy candidates (otherwise you wouldn't have offered them a job). But 50 percent is still an astonishingly high number.

This is the position Ashley Unwin found himself in while a senior partner at Deloitte in the UK, so he asked his team to investigate. A series of interviews with candidates who had declined offers soon revealed a pattern. The recruitment process was so overly analytical that there was no place for any *emotion*. Candidates left the interview feeling that the firm was candid but clinical, with little laughter, passion, or enthusiasm. The interviewers clicked into "interview mode," forensically probing and testing for candidates' strengths, weaknesses, and cultural fit, but they failed to demonstrate the passion *they* had for the company.

Candidates were not helped into a state of mind that psychologists call "positive affect." Simply put, "positive affect" is about being in a positive mood. Our mood shapes how we think about almost every situation we encounter. According to Alice Isen from Cornell University, positive affect facilitates a host of good outcomes, including our openness to information, creativity, cognitive flexibility, and ability to respond innovatively.[13]

Failing to create positive affect was turning off highly talented candidates. In the end, to address this issue, the company made a subtle but significant change to their recruitment process. All interviewers were told that, at some convenient point in their interviews, they had to take a time-out from asking questions and spend five minutes talking about themselves. They were asked to introduce the discussion with the following words "let me tell you why I love working here."

That was it. Nothing else.

By teeing-up a discussion in this way, the interviewers were given an opportunity to demonstrate the passion they had for the business, its culture, and its people. The interviewer showed their own positive affect, and through emotional contagion, it helped the candidates to feel excited themselves. This one change had an immediate impact: acceptance rates jumped to around 80% almost overnight.

This is just one example of how to make people feel good at a moment that matters. To replicate this success, leaders must recognise these moments and figure out ways to respond to them so they can deliver positive affect for their people. Another useful tactic can be to frame the moment as a milestone or transition (they often are). When it comes to a reset, such moments of transition can be hugely valuable. To identify and design an effective moment that matters for your employees, try the following steps.

Step One: Map Your Employee Journey

Consider the big, important moments in an employee's experience and break them down into more granular steps. A very basic journey map for a typical employee could look something like the one shown in Table 3.2:

Table 3.2 Employee Journey Map

Source, Select, & On-board	Perform, Engage, Develop	Mobility & Exit
Apply to job advert	Agree objectives and targets	Go on secondment
Attend interview	Attend formal training	Gain cycles of experience
Conduct tests	Receive coaching & mentoring	Receive promotion
Receive job offer	Attend conferences & awaydays	Take annual leave
Day 1 induction	Deliver meaningful work	Change working patterns
Meet line manager	Receive formal rewards	Voluntary exit
Induction journey	Receive informal recognition	Retirement

Notice how each of the granular steps represents a moment of emotional expectation. These moments provide opportunities to elevate and delight and therefore increase enthusiasm throughout your organisation. Organisations' failure to raise these moments above the routine is staggering, not to mention a real missed opportunity. It's possible to gather data via employee surveys to establish the satisfaction with each of these moments or, better, to conduct a driver analysis to establish which moment has the biggest impact on overall levels of seeking system activation.

Step Two: Design the Moment

When trying to create positive affect, a number of key factors should be considered during the design of the employee experience and moment elevation:

- **Introduce novelty**. When elevating moments, novelty is important. Our dopamine levels rise as soon as we detect something unexpected, so try and build a positive surprise into the design of the moment.
- **Dial up your own enthusiasm.** If you, as a leader, are involved in making the moment memorable, don't forget the power of emotional contagion (discussed in Chapter 2). Ensure your own seeking system is fully engaged to be prepared for the right moments. Notice how, in the Deloitte example, the interviewers' seeking systems were engaged by talking about their *own* passions and purpose. Emotional contagion ensured that those positive emotions were "caught" by the candidate.
- **Create theatre:** Moments can be elevated when people dress up for them or introduce props to indicate their significance. Take the example of the induction process at machinery company John Deere, as described by Stanford Professor Chip Heath and his brother Dan, a senior fellow at Duke University's CASE center, in their book *The Power of Moments*.[14] New employees are led through a highly choreographed welcome over several days, including being led to their new desk, which has been dressed with a welcome banner. John Deere knows that new employees are emotionally vulnerable, and by attending to this moment that matters, they are enabled to feel a sense of belonging, causing them to start doing better work sooner.
- **Involve employees in the experience:** While we can feel enthusiastic by passively observing an experience that is unexpected, funny, and appeals to our senses, our enthusiasm soars when we are immersed in an experience that includes positive social interactions, otherwise known as audience participation. For example, a food delivery service identified a weekly meeting between delivery drivers and their managers – known as the "roundsman's debrief" – as a moment that mattered in the employee experience. During those meetings, managers began asking their drivers "How can I help you deliver excellent service?" This simple servant leadership question transformed the meetings into two-way, adult-to-adult, positive problem-solving dialogues.

Step Three: Obsess About the Moment

When elevating moments, it's best to focus on one moment at a time, and to persevere with its design and execution. Otherwise, it's easy to water down an elevated moment. The effort required to provide the theatre, novelty, and involvement required can be easily challenged in the name of efficiency. It's only by providing the right amount of attention density that you will make the moment a success and realise the benefits. Similarly, having ten "moments that matter" also dilutes the effort and can result in key moments falling depressingly flat.

Summary

- To activate our seeking systems, we need to first reset, reducing our cognitive load and regulating our emotions to attain a state of focused curiosity.
- By reducing distractions through processes such as simplification and prioritisation, leaders are able to help their team members reduce their cognitive load, allowing them to identify and attend to what matters most.
- Another way to reduce cognitive load is by increasing focus, a process by which goal clarity helps us to prioritise what is important, and normalising focus time allows us to work effectively on those important tasks.
- Anxiety can be reduced creating psychological safety, a belief that we will not be punished or humiliated for speaking up with our ideas, questions, or concerns, or for making mistakes. The leadership behaviours required to cue safety across an enterprise are encapsulated in the 3 Cs framework, which encourages leaders to consult with others, consider ideas and feedback, and provide closure on the agreed way forward.
- Feeling more positive emotions can help in reaching a state of focused curiosity, and this can be achieved by elevating key moments in the employee experience.

Notes

1   Schwab, K. (2020) "The Great Rest." *World Economic Forum*, June 3.
2   As quoted in Zen and the Art of Stand-up Comedy (1998) by Jay Sankey.

3   Rogelberg, S. G., and L. Kreamer (2019) The Case for More Silence in Meetings. *Harvard Business Review* 97, no. 2: 2–5. https://hbr.org/2019/06/the-case-for-more-silence-in-meetings

4   www.themuse.com/advice/how-much-time-do-we-spend-in-meetings-hint-its-scary

5   Lütke, T. (2016) *The Observer Effect*. Eleanor Taylor. www.theobservereffect.org/tobi.html

6   PBS (2009) "Clifford Nass." Interviews – Clifford Nass | Digital Nation | FRONT-LINE | PBS.

7   Schwartz, Tony, Jean Gomes, and Catherine McCarthy (2010, May 18) *The Way We're Working Isn't Working: The Four Forgotten Needs That Energize Great Performance*. New York: Simon & Schuster.

8   Schwartz, T. (2011) "A 90-Minute Plan for Personal Effectiveness." *Harvard Business Review*. Body breaks and the 90-minute mark | INTHEBLACK.

9   London Business School (2021) "Why Time is the Currency of Knowledge Work." *Forbes*, May 4, 2021. Why Time Is The Currency Of Knowledge Work (forbes.com).

10 Edmondson, Amy C., and Zhike Lei. "Psychological safety: the history, renaissance, and future of an interpersonal construct." *Annual Review of Organizational Psychology and Organizational Behavior* 1, no. 1 (2014): 23–43.

11 Detert, J. R., and E. Burris (2016) "Can Your Employees Really Speak Freely?" *Harvard Business Review* (January-February): 80–87. https://hbr.org/2016/01/can-your-employees-really-speak-freely

12 Is it safe to speak up at work? WorkLife podcast with Adam Grant, 20 July 2021.

13 Isen, Alice M. (1987) "Positive affect, cognitive processes, and social behavior." In *Advances in Experimental Social Psychology* (vol. 20, pp. 203–253). Cambridge, Massachusetts: Academic Press.

14 Heath, Chip, and Dan Heath (2019) *The Power of Moments: Why Certain Experiences Have Extraordinary Impact*. London: Corgi, pp. 20–22.

Building the Frame

"Professional Services" involves a range of different occupations that provide support to businesses in the form of advice or service roles. To say it's a huge industry is an understatement: professional services firms in the United States generated nearly $2 trillion in combined revenue in 2019 (a 5 percent increase from 2018).[1] That same year, the US industry included 9.4 million jobs spread out over 1.2 million firms. In the UK, it's estimated that professional services make up 13% of all UK employment, 25% of all businesses, and add £190bn to the economy.[2]

Time is the primary unit of cost and value for the vast majority of professional services firms. Client-facing employees must therefore track their time so costs can be allocated and bills raised. The most common metric for client-facing staff is known as "utilisation," the percent of total hours per week that is billable to clients. If you are client-facing, then a high utilisation means you are in-demand and earning revenues for the firm. If you take on a more senior role, however, your measures of success change. What becomes increasingly important to you is selling new projects and ensuring the portfolio of projects you manage are profitable.

This system creates a tension between leaders' and employees' incentives. On most contracts, leaders are incentivised to control the number of hours booked to complete the work, as the fewer hours are recorded, the higher the project margin. Staff, on the other hand, want to recognise every hour they work on a project so to maximise their personal utilisation. While there is typically some give and take between leaders and employees, in the long run the system tends to favour the leaders due to their positional power. Not wanting to get on the wrong side of their boss, most workers end

DOI: 10.4324/9781003396833-7

up booking fewer hours than they actually work. The true profitability of projects gets hidden, as not all time spent on the project is recorded, and the business may continue to sell and invest in an unprofitable line of work. This path can lead to burnout as staff are loaded with more and more work due to having apparent availability, when in reality, they may have been working 12-hour days for weeks.

What we see here are leaders struggling with what they consider a trade-off between optimising their own performance metrics and keeping their employees engaged and delivering their best work. If leaders push too hard, eventually the status quo becomes unsustainable as burnout soars, and management decides to make a big push for more honest timekeeping. This can take different forms, but usually results in a dictate. For example, mandates for inflexible rules could be put in place: "We now expect you to record every hour you work. If you are discouraged from doing so, please raise this with senior management." Or a set of simple rules and principles can be established, such as both manager and employee mutually agreeing on budgeted hours that should not be exceeded.

When working life – so full of paradox and dilemmas – reaches a point where a particular practice becomes unsustainable, leaders often respond by imposing some strict new rules, hoping to create a reset by "jolting" the organisation into a better way of doing things. But telling employees to talk to management when they feel discouraged to book the actual hours they've worked doesn't fix the core problem. Instead, the mandate triggers a threat response, dampening the seeking system and failing to create the state of focused curiosity so important for a reset. What is more, the organisational problems that triggered leadership's response in the first place tend to return in time. There has to be a better way.

What is needed for a long-term reset is a common understanding of an operational framework that balances individual or business-unit freedoms with the ability to effectively deliver on client commitments. Of course, this framework doesn't just apply to professional services. A well-constructed frame can provide the psychological reset needed to help solve the paradox between individual satisfaction and overall effi-ciency in any organisation. To do so, the frame must be made explicit, kept under constant review, and change in real time as necessary. To see how to apply this idea in your own organisation, let's start by taking a closer look at the concept of an operational frame introduced in the previous chapters.

The Frame

The frame refers to what organisations need to do to survive and thrive. In order to scale, organisations need employees to meet regulations, deliver on promises to customers, and not hurt the organisation as they experiment and learn. The frame allows an organisation to know whether or not it is adapting and winning. The goal of leaders is to work with employees so everyone clearly understands the frame – and what is meant by "winning" – and then help them find the freedom within that frame.

As a reminder, freedom within the frame refers to the space where employees can experiment, express themselves, and play to their strengths to help the organisation succeed (recall the Blame Bruce policy from Chapter 1). This freedom is only possible when employees understand the organisational frame and the shared purpose of the work they're performing. The right tension between the freedom and the frame will help activate employees' seeking systems and direct their enthusiasm toward solving organisational problems. Building a frame is useful on multiple levels. It can be used to reset a simple meeting, for a thorny business problem (such as honest timekeeping), or for an entire organisational strategy.

While every organisational frame is different, it is broadly made up of four main boundary conditions, as shown in Figure 4.1:

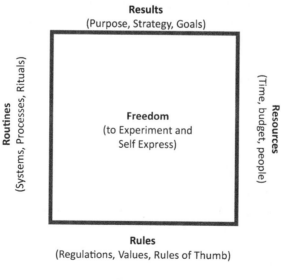

Figure 4.1

Organisational Frame

The four R's of the organisational frame are results, resources, routines, and rules. Each of these must be made explicit. As shown, *results* are made up of purpose, strategy, and goals; *resources* are time constraints, budgets, and people; *rules* consist of regulations, values, rules of thumb, and the like; and *routines* include systems, processes, and rituals (more on rituals in Chapter 8). The frame should be developed and discussed with every member of a team. This is not to say every team member should always be given a choice about all aspects of the frame – some elements will need to be mandated (for example, budgets may not be flexible, or values must be kept) – but it's important that everyone has an opportunity to deepen their understanding of the frame, align on a common understanding of its boundary conditions, and learn to constantly question and challenge it.

Peak performance is achieved only when the operational frame is fully understood. Even when a frame is well articulated, it can be perceived in different ways depending on how each individual interprets it. To some, a small team with limited resources may be viewed as a constraint; to others, it can be viewed as an enabler for quicker and more agile decision-making. Misalignment between team members is a major cause of poor performance. Only through exploration with all team members does the frame become apparent and can common understanding be reached. Therefore, one of the most important jobs of a leader is helping groups that need to work together to gain a shared understanding of the operational frame.

The Frame in Action

The best way to learn how to build a frame is by example. Let's imagine you work for a professional services firm, like one of those mentioned earlier in the chapter. You are the head of a consulting business and are currently experiencing problems associated with the lack of accurate timekeeping. You have discussed the issue at your leadership team meetings but have never reached consensus on how to address the full extent of the problem. You decide to convene a 90-minute meeting with your leadership team to specifically address the issue, and send your team a memo to set it up:

To: Heads of Public Sector Consulting, Financial Sector Consulting, and Private Sector Consulting, Heads of Finance, Operations, and HR

Subject Line: Timesheets and their Business Impact

Dear Team,

We have discussed the issue of inaccurate time recording and looked anecdotally at its impact on our business. We have all observed examples of staff burnout, despite relatively low utilisation rates, and how the data on the true performance of different consulting offerings is unreliable due to this timekeeping issue.

I recognise that competing pressures may mean the answer may not be as simple as mandating "book every hour you work," but we owe it to our staff, and our overall business, to provide better guidance on this issue.

I would like to convene a 90 minute meeting for our leadership team where we can discuss and agree to an approach moving forward. Suggested objectives and agenda below. Invite to follow.

Objectives
- Explore the issue of accurate time-keeping
- Plan how we are going to solve/manage the problem

Agenda
- State objectives
- Agree to ground rules for the meeting
- Review data over time
- Build the frame
  - Results
  - Resources
  - Routines
  - Rules
- Challenge the frame
- Agree to next steps

Regards,
Your team leader

Note that by sending out the objectives and agenda in advance – and by discussing these and the ground rules at the start of the meeting – you have actually built an operational frame *for the meeting itself*. You have provided clarity on results (the objectives), resources (attendees and the 90-minute duration), routines (the agenda), and rules (the behavioural ground rules for the meeting). This simple process helps attendees get into the state of focused curiosity needed for a reset and to set up a successful meeting.

When the meeting is underway, you begin by explaining the accurate time-keeping issue as a complex challenge requiring *collective* effort. Using a technique discussed in Chapter 3, when talking about the meeting objectives you focus the group on the benefits of the solution by saying that clear guidance on time recording will allow your people to perform at their best and give the leadership team better data on the company's performance. This explanation is meant to get the problem out in the open, prime a solution-focused mindset, and head off any potential issues with your leadership team, who may otherwise immediately become defensive in an effort to protect their "turf."

You explain to the team that agreeing to the operational framework is a mechanism to both deepen the understanding of the problem and to identify potential solutions. Agreeing to the frame will provide not only your team but the whole business with clear boundaries, plus an understanding of the freedom they have to operate within the frame.

You then ask the team about the ground rules: "How should we all act and behave in the meeting to make it a success?"

You write down their responses:

- "Well, I guess we should all keep an open mind as we explore the problem."
- "Let's think through the implications of any suggestions for improvement."
- "We should try not to be defensive – we may find some of our own behaviours have contributed to this issue."
- "Yes, and we must be honest with each other – let's make explicit the assumptions we all hold about what we think is valued around here, and how it impacts our behaviour."

You capture these ground rules on a flip chart and make your own commitment to abide by them during the meeting. You then ask everyone for a show of hands as to their commitment. By taking this step, you have made these self-identified behaviours relevant, available, and public – essential ingredients if the team members are to follow through on their commitment.

Next up on the agenda: reviewing key data points over time. You refer to collected data that you had issued as a pre-read to the meeting. To ground the team in the current reality, you include any previous leadership interventions that have taken place, along with their results. In this case the following data is available:

Measure	Performance over time
Group utilisation	Very gradual rise from 52% to 59% during the course of the year. Still under the 65% utilisation target.
Resourcing	Managers report increasing difficulty finding resources to work on their projects. Consultants claim they are busy even when their personal utilisation rates are low.
Group revenue	Started the year on budget; now improved 6% above budget.
Group profitability	Remaining steady at 38% gross profit.
Consistency of time-booking guidance	Anecdotal data only: guidance is not written down or consistently communicated by leaders. Unwritten rules seem to be to minimise time booked to increase margin on fixed price projects (or provide some wiggle room if the work takes longer than planned).
Employee engagement	Increasing complaints of burnout. Consultants juggling too many projects. "Complexity of business processes" highlighted as an improvement area on the annual engagement survey for the third year running.
Sickness rates	Spiked in the last two months.
Success of previous interventions	Two years previously you ran a communications campaign on the importance of "honest timekeeping" and why this was important for the business. After an initial improvement, the problem has now returned worse than ever.
"Non chargeable" time booking	Analysis shows that non-chargeable hours are booked mainly to "business development" (60%) and "Admin" (35%).

After discussing the data and its possible causes, everyone in the meeting agrees it suggests inconsistencies in how time is being booked. People are clearly busy. Group utilisation is increasing, and it is getting harder to secure resources for projects. The rise in sickness rates coincides with the employee survey, which shows evidence of increased psychological exhaustion and burnout, reinforcing that many people are working very hard. At the same time, however, group utilisation levels are still below target and while some internal projects are occupying employees' time, these are not time consuming enough to result in the below target utilisation. With revenues ahead of budget and a flat margin, you conclude that, overall, not all billable time is being allocated as it should.

You discuss the assumptions people hold about booking their time and hypothesise that these assumptions are many and varied. In the absence of consistent guidance from leadership, staff are probably making their own assumptions about the "rules" for booking their time. The failure of previous interventions to have a long-term impact also suggests that even when people *do* feel clear about the rules, they are unwilling to follow them for long.

Having agreed that a problem exists, it is time to start building the frame to help manage this workplace dilemma. You draw-up the following template on a flip chart:

Building the Frame

Results	
What's our purpose as an organisation/team?	What's our strategy to succeed?
What's our objective right now?	
How will we know we've met our objective?	
Resources	
Which people are available to help us achieve our objective?	What budget do we have to achieve our objective?
How much time do we have available to achieve our objective?	
Routines	
What systems must we use?	What processes must we adhere to?
What rituals should we change/introduce?	
Rules	
How will we work together, based on our values?	What are the regulatory rules?
What simple rules of thumb exist?	What unwritten rules exist?

To develop your frame, always start with the results. Without a clear vision of success, you and your workforce may have to undergo a hard, and often painful, process without anyone really understanding the point. You can set context by discussing your firm's purpose and strategy. You should then discuss, and agree on, the creative challenge or mission you face right now. Note the focus on your goal, rather than your problem. This focus is important because it primes our brains to notice information relevant to the solution we are hoping to discover, puts us in a state of focused curiosity, and enables a reset that helps activate our seeking system. We want to move toward the solution rather than avoid the problem.

In this case, as the conversation develops, you align on the following:

Results	
What's our purpose as an organisation/team? *We help our clients address the human side of transformational change. We aim to unleash the potential of our clients' employees.*	What's our strategy to succeed? *We target mid-cap organisations looking to grow. Our strategy is to grow with our clients, developing deep relationships and working with them over the long term. This strategy results in bigger engagements with a smaller number of clients more often. We offer research backed by practical solutions that deliver value quickly.*
What's our objective right now? *We want more accurate time recording data in order to make better business decisions about:* • *Employee well-being* • *Resourcing* • *Employee development* • *Business performance & strategy (including by business unit, product, and geography)*	
How will we know we've met our objective? • *Utilisation data will better reflect how many hours employees actually spend on client work* • *Employee engagement scores will increase* • *Sickness days will decrease* • *We will be delivering on our strategy (winning more large projects with fewer clients, and the average number of projects any consultant is working on at one time will be reduced)*	

Using the template as a structure for the conversation brings clarity to the situation. You find that by deepening relationships with fewer clients and winning more, large-scale projects, consultants will work on fewer projects at the same time. Since there is typically a degree of "admin" necessary on any project – and consultants often feel unjustified in charging this time to a client job code – the fewer projects they work on, the less "admin" time will go uncharged. By setting context and discussing purpose and strategy, you and the group have now come to realise that executing firm strategy will also help manage the issue of honest timekeeping.

An unintended consequence of this discussion is that it has helped strengthen the resolve of the leadership team behind the firm's strategy. The strategy has therefore become a part of the "frame" to help achieve the goal of more accurate time recording.

Next, you discuss the resources that are available to achieve the sought-after results and conclude the following:

Resources	
Which people are available to help us achieve our objective?	What budget do we have to achieve our objective?
All employees have personal responsibility to submit accurate timesheets.	*Some budget must be allowed for any process or technology changes required to drive the desired behaviours. (This will be returned to once potential solutions are proposed.)*
All members of the leadership team need to role model accurate timekeeping and consistently communicate the agreed upon messaging.	
The problem should be "owned" by all members of the leadership team but the head of operations should take the lead.	
How much time do we have available to achieve our objective?	
Some visible changes – to process, communications, and behaviours – need to be made within one month. Looking for full systemic change within three months and sustainable changes to key metrics within six months.	

The resources step forces a conversation about timescales and ownership. At this stage the team are committed to the goal and have assigned responsibilities. Now it's time to look at the third wall of the frame: routines.

The discussion leads the team to think through existing working practices and how employees currently think about them. The team considers the main questions staff brought up during the interviews:

- Typically, jobs are costed to clients on a "day rate" basis (not on hourly rates). If we work all day on a client's project but spend one hour during the day doing necessary client admin, should that hour also be charged to the client?
- The cost of every hour booked is charged to a project at a full cost rate. We are not paid overtime, therefore if more than eight hours are booked in a given day, the "cost" allocated to that code is not strictly accurate. If we work ten hours in a day rather than the contracted eight, should the extra hours be charged?
- If we work fewer than our contracted eight hours in a day, as we need to attend to a personal issue, the system doesn't currently allow us to record fewer than eight hours. Currently, we just make up the time on subsequent days so it evens out over the week. Is that OK?
- A natural tension exists between doing the best for the client (going "over and above" without charging more), the best for the business and our managers (delivering under the allocated hours to maximise profitability), and the best for ourselves (maximising our own hours billed – utilisation – our main measure of success). How do we ensure consistency in our approach?
- Sometimes no clear job code exists for how we have been spending our time, even though it is still legitimate. For example, one of us may take initiative and seek to improve an internal process. In the absence of a non-chargeable code, what should we book such time to? Typically, it currently goes to "admin" or "business development."
- Sometimes we have to work long and unsociable hours on a critical project. Can we take any time off to make up for this extra work?
- Often, all our necessary admin, career development, and learning takes place *after* spending a full day on client projects. How should we record this time when the norm is to just record those eight hours per day?

As you discuss the issues, the leadership team keeps returning to the desired results, asking themselves what routines would help to achieve them. Considering employee well-being, resourcing, employee development, and business strategy and performance, it becomes clear that while consistency and guidance are needed, the process must also allow for some judgement and flexibility. To be too prescriptive would be to remove any freedom within the frame, dampening the seeking system. Together, you settle on the following:

Routines	
What systems must we use?	What processes must we adhere to?
The company uses a time-recording system that directly feeds the company accounts.	*Employees are required to code their own time to timesheets at the end of every working week.*
We will update the system such that up to eight hours per day can be charged to appropriate codes.	*Employees should feel free to exercise judgement about the spread of hours over the week as long as:*
Time over and above eight hours should be charged to a "shadow" code. This code does not attract utilisation or cost, but it allows all *time to be recorded, creating the ability to better monitor employee well-being.*	• *The weekly hours reflect time spent on the client's project during that week.* • *All hours worked are recorded (with any hours over 40 per week recorded to "shadow" codes).* • *Client work should always take priority in the 40-hour time booking window.*
What rituals should we change/introduce?	
We will stop the ritual shaming of individuals who have booked more time to a project than expected. Each project leader will introduce a monthly "after-action review" to include a review of project finances and a focus on learning.	

The final part of the frame is concerned with rules. The team discusses regulatory rules, unwritten rules (a proxy for your culture), and any simple rules or guidelines that should be provided. The summary discussion is captured in the template below:

Rules	
How will we work together, based on our values?	What are the regulatory rules?
Our values as a business are to act with integrity, care for each other and our clients, make a difference, collaborate, and innovate.	*In order to remain compliant with Directive 2003/88/EC or Working Time Directive (WTD), evidence must be provided that employees receive at least four weeks in paid holidays each year, rest breaks, and rest of at least 11 hours in any 24 hours. Excessive night work must be restricted; a day off after a week's work provided; and employees should work no more than 48 hours per week over an average of 17 weeks.*
Making our values salient, especially those of integrity and care, will help to guide decisions around accurate timekeeping.	

Rules	
What simple rules of thumb exist?	What unwritten rules exist?
No written or consistent guidance currently exists. As leaders, we will consistently communicate the following: • *"Book all the hours you work in a week, but use judgement and flexibility on daily bookings."* • *"Use shadow codes for any hours worked above 40 hours per week."* • *"If you feel under any pressure to book time in a way that is not consistent with our organisation's values, speak to the COO."*	*Needs to be verified with staff, but we currently assume:* • *Employees record time in a way that makes them look as good as possible to their project leader.* • *Employees don't book more than their contracted 40 hours per week.* *Need to address these unwritten rules such that:* • *Booking all hours is an accepted practice.* • *Some freedom and flexibility exists so that hours balance over the course of a week.*

With the rules established, the initial frame is now complete. You and the leadership team start to test the frame by discussing the amount of freedom that should be afforded to employees in order to achieve the desired results. Some feel the frame needs to be tightened to provide simple but strict rules of behaviour. Others point out that this hasn't worked in the past and is unlikely to work now. They argue for a more relaxed approach based on principles and consistent communication.

As a general rule, value lies in exploring the creative tension between the operational frame and employees' ability to experiment and express themselves in service of organisational goals. If the framework is too tight, a "learned helplessness" kicks in, where a lack of autonomy and control dampens the seeking system. This causes the organisation to miss out on the collective energy and genius of the employees. If the framework is too loose, however, employees lack focus, consistency, and creative challenge.

The best way to create this tension is to challenge the frame – the fourth step on the agenda – and question how the team thinks about it. A great exercise for doing this, and one that the team now uses, is called "Enablers or Constraints."

Exercise: Enablers or Constraints

What Is It?

An exercise to encourage teams to challenge the frame, with the intention of removing constraints where possible. For example, some team members may consider the simple rule *"Book all the hours you work in a week, but use judgement and flexibility on daily bookings"* to be a constraint. For them, specifying a weekly timeframe does not provide a big enough time horizon for required flexibility. Others may consider the time horizon as a necessary part of the frame – an enabler – to reinforce the importance of booking all hours at every timesheet submission. This exercise allows for that debate.

How Long Does It Take?

Forty-five minutes to one hour, depending on the size of the group.

Group Size?

Small groups of typically five to ten, such as a leadership team responsible for the business challenge at hand.

How Does It Work?

Individuals within the group are each given the completed template that resulted from building the frame together. Next, they are asked to draw two circles on a piece of paper, labelling them "constraints" and "enablers," as shown in Figure 4.2.

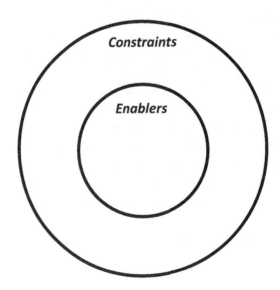

Figure 4.2

Enablers and Constraints

Working individually, participants now spend 20 minutes mapping the elements of the operational frame into the diagram, including everything that has been written out on the template. Those aspects of the frame they consider "enablers" are shown in the inner circle; those they consider "constraints" are shown in the outer circle. Next, the meeting leader will ask the participants to share their diagrams. In almost all circumstances, people will have listed different items in each ring of the circle. Some aspects of the framework that are seen as constraints by certain team members will be seen as enablers by others. These differences should then be actively discussed, creating a conversation around whether or not any changes should be made to the frame, which is often the outcome of the exercise. From there, everyone needs to agree on how to move forward.

A common understanding of the creative tension that exists at the frame boundaries has now been established, along with a fresh understanding of how constraints can, in fact, yield benefits in achieving the business challenge. Your team may also realise that a constraint can be relaxed, removed, or changed. Either of these outcomes is good for the seeking system, providing more space – an expanded frame – to allow for self-expression and experimentation.

Bringing the Frame to the People

After you and your team understand and agree on the frame, you now need to communicate it with your employees. In the case of the specific but tricky time-recording issue, this may be as straightforward as a written communication about the simple rules that need to be followed, which are then role modelled and consistently communicated by leaders. In the case of a more macro level frame concerning a new project or company strategy, it pays to ask your employees to challenge the frame and ask them about how they want to contribute to it.

These conversations are how servant leadership works. Rather than trying to motivate employees to do things in pre-decided ways, the goal of a leader is to serve others as they try to improve the company and grow in their jobs. In this way, leaders act humbly, remaining open to learning from employees about what metrics and feedback would be helpful. Think of these discussions as a way to practice and model humility with employees, allowing both leaders and followers to be more receptive to new ideas, criticism, or changes in the external environment.

Summary

- Many leaders attempt to reset their organisation by imposing new draconian rules. However, this can provoke a threat response and does not provide the state of focused curiosity required for seeking system ignition.
- Creating a clear understanding of the "freedom in the frame" for employees is a powerful strategy to reset. The frame consists of four "Rs": *results, resources, routines,* and *rules*.
- The desired *results* come from an understanding of your firm's purpose and strategy, focusing on the creative challenge that stands in the way between your organisation and the desired goals.
- *Resources* are the time constraints, budgets, and people involved in any given project that help or hinder achieving the desired goals.
- *Routines* include systems, processes, and rituals – whether explicitly stated or not – that affect an organisation's day-to-day activities and their ability to achieve the desired goals.
- *Rules* consist of regulations, values, rules of thumb, and any other similar elements that create further structure to the frame.
- Freedom within the frame, a necessary aspect for resetting and activating seeking systems, occurs only when employees understand the organisational frame and the shared purpose of the work they're performing.

Notes

1 SelectUSA Professional Services Industry (trade.gov).
2 PBS (2021) "5 key trends for professional services." *Allianz.co.uk,* April, 27.

PART 3

Ignite

Discovering Insight

In 1965 it was almost impossible to reliably air freight goods to other parts of mainland US in fewer than two to three days. So when Yale undergraduate Frederick W. Smith wrote a term paper outlining a system to accommodate urgent, time-sensitive shipments of goods such as medicine, computer parts, and electronics, he was excited by the possibilities to address this unmet need. Unconvinced by the economic implications, however, Smith's professor only gave the paper an average grade. Fast forward 56 years, and that average thesis changed the history of the courier services industry, resulting in the $84 billion behemoth that is FedEx.[1]

From its earliest days, FedEx has had a strong sense of purpose, connecting people and possibilities around the world. When Joe Anthamatten joined the company in 1998, he already held a strong belief in that purpose. The company was big on "culture fit," and throughout Joe's recruitment process, it was clear the company was full of people like him – hardworking, committed to collaborative teamwork, and fun to be around. Joe felt that this was the team for him, and he became as committed to the idea of "the golden package" – treating every package as if it were made of gold – as other employees across the FedEx family.

Joe worked for FedEx Services, a branch of the company providing HR, finance, procurement, and other "back-office" services to the front line. He loved his work and considered himself a true carrier of the FedEx culture. But, after years of rapid business growth, delivering seamless and effective back-office services was becoming increasingly difficult. The back-office functions of all newly acquired businesses had joined FedEx Services, which had grown from 6,000 to 20,000 employees. Inconsistent working practices and different cultural norms were creeping in, which was making the

DOI: 10.4324/9781003396833-9

business more bureaucratic and difficult to manage. As Joe says, "there is a fine line between a groove and a rut," and it was clear that the culture required some attention.

FedEx Services retained a consulting firm to guide them through a culture shaping journey. According to Joe, by far the most impactful part of that journey was a two-day workshop designed to provide insights into how individuals and teams were behaving. These workshops were highly experiential, using exercises and personal stories from participants to uncover existing behavioural patterns. Reflecting on, and then sharing, these stories and experiences created the conditions for insights about individual and team behaviour. These insights could then help to ignite the participants' seeking systems and act as a catalyst for change.

These workshops were rolled out to 20 people at a time across the whole organisation, over a period of 18 months. In time, sales and productivity improved, new product development cycles came down, customer complaints dropped, and employee engagement soared. Joe and his colleagues realised that the key to the change lay in effective insight generation for every individual in the company. As he put it, "If the soil is healthy, anything can grow."

Insight is a point in time when you achieve an "Aha!" moment. This deep and sudden realisation makes you look at a situation, a problem, yourself, or even the world in a different way. New thought patterns appear, or seem to appear, in an instant, like the flick of a light switch, and new neural networks are created. The resulting emotional rush we experience is the moment in which our seeking systems are ignited. But new insights are unlikely to occur if the conditions aren't right. Therefore, you must create the appropriate conditions for people throughout your organisation to have more meaningful insights, more often. To do so at scale, you can implement two main strategies: encouraging experiential learning and introducing pattern disrupts. Both aim to ensure that, like Joe Anthamatten at FedEx, you create healthy soil in which the people you lead can truly grow.

Encourage Experiential Learning

Psychologist and educational theorist David Kolb's theory of experiential learning proposes that the opportunity to reflect on our experiences is vital to the learning process and the ability to create insights.[2] By reflecting on the learning activities we participate in, we no longer just focus on the *how* of the task but also on the *why*. The experiential learning cycle shown in Figure 5.1 has been adapted from Kolb's work, and a social peer sharing component has been added which I have found essential for team and organisational learning, as well as enhancing the individual's experience. For learning to be effective, the learner must progress through this cycle of five stages:

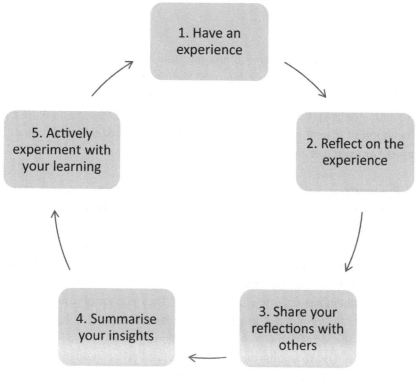

Figure 5.1
The Experiential Learning Cycle

Notice how the cycle embodies all the triggers of the seeking system: reflecting on the experience, including the "why" of your work (personalised purpose), sharing with others (self-expression), and trying out what you have learned (experimentation). But without reflection, there are fewer opportunities for insight to occur, and the learning experience itself may have been all for not.

Many business leaders are aware of the importance of reflection for their employees yet struggle to encourage people to actually do it. While most employees see it as a good idea, the pressure of the next deadline often means that reflective practices are ignored. The trick is to embed a number of simple work routines and then make them a habit, a part of your organisational culture. There are a number of strategies that support the experiential learning cycle, including scheduling reviews, setting learning goals, and encouraging storytelling.

Schedule Reviews

While reflective practices are commonly built into learning and development programs, they are less often used during day-to day-operations. Two well-known tools – one to use before a significant piece of work and one to use after – help to normalise the use of reflective practices and increase the likelihood of insight (note that "a significant piece of work" could mean a project or even just a period of time):

- **Pre-mortems.** This method, first devised by Gary Klein,[3] imagines how a project might fail or succeed in order to anticipate risks and avoid potential issues. While a post-mortem review of a project after it ends allows you to learn from mistakes, a pre-mortem increases your chances of avoiding them in the first place, plus it ignites the seeking system though visualisation of project success. They typically only last 60–90 minutes, and they involve members of a new project team. They consist of a project overview, a brainstorm of possible project failures and successes that generates insight, and development of an action plan. Discuss questions such as: What could make us miss our project deadline? What could make us blow our budget? What would make us deliver a poor-quality project? What are you nervous about? What has gone wrong on previous projects? Such brainstorming helps teams have new insights about risks at the outset, such that they can plan for their mitigation and prevent them from occurring. In fact, research by Deborah J. Mitchell of the Wharton School; Jay Russo of Cornell; and Nancy Pennington of the University of Colorado found that asking "What could go wrong with this plan?" resulted in a 30 percent improvement in predicting the outcomes.[4]
- **After Action Reviews (AARs).** AARs are a simple tool that facilitates continuous learning by bringing together a team to discuss a completed task,

event, activity, or project in an open and honest way. First developed by the U.S. Army,[5] the essence of an AAR is to think about an experience immediately after it has occurred in order to allow reflection and the generation of insights that can be applied to future activities. There are many different ways to conduct AARs, but the whole process should be kept as simple and as easy to remember as possible. Simplicity and ease allow you to apply AARs in different contexts, becoming a core part of how you do business. Immediately after a task, event, activity, or project, preferably while you are still immersed in the environment where the work took place, ask your team to reflect on the following: What was supposed to happen? What actually happened? Why were there differences? What worked? What didn't? Why? What would you do differently next time?

Pre-mortems and AARs are two types of reviews that create the chance for reflection, but there are others to consider. For example, reflective practice can be built into feedback by asking the recipient to reflect on how they felt about a particular event before providing your own view. No matter which type of review you choose to incorporate into your business activity, make sure they build space for regular, consistent reflection.

Set Learning Goals

Learning goals are used extensively in educational settings and typically define what students should be able to understand, identify, or define at the end of a learning period. If you are an English teacher, for example, you may consider your course a success if, when complete, your students are able to:

- Apply critical terms and methodology in completing a literary analysis following the conventions of standard written English.
- Locate, apply, and cite effective secondary materials in their own texts.
- Analyse and interpret texts within the contexts they are written.

These specific objectives make sense when your "product" is learning, but what about other types of business? Most organisations' prime focus is on achievement or "performance" goals (what you do) and sometimes "behavioural" goals (how you do it). They struggle to systematically set explicit learning goals (what you need to learn), even though these are also essential for building a culture of insight.

A learning goal is framed in terms of acquisition of knowledge or skill – such as "discover three strategies to generate more leads" – drawing attention away from the end result to the discovery of effective task processes. Learning goals are best set at the beginning of a performance period, whether starting a new project or beginning a performance review cycle. They should be agreed to by both employees and their leaders as part of a regular coaching conversation (see Chapter 10 for more details).

Let's say you are starting a new role as manager of a project team tasked with identifying ways for your company to reach net-zero carbon emissions. What does the team need to learn to deliver a successful performance outcome? To uncover and set effective learning goals, you could pose the following questions to their employees:

- "What are the most important concepts – such as ideas, methods, theories, approaches, perspectives, and other broad themes of your field – you should be able to understand, identify, or define at the end of the learning period?"
- "What questions should you be able to answer at the end of the learning period?"
- "What are the most important skills you should develop and be able to apply during and after the learning period?"
- "How can I help you build these skills and test your mastery of these skills?"

Only once employees have the knowledge and behavioural skills necessary to perform the task should a specific performance goal be set. The performance goal then cues individuals to use the strategies and skills they know are effective.

Encourage Storytelling

Storytelling is a traditional and ancient means of passing on wisdom and culture, and its value in business has been increasingly recognised by business leaders in recent years. A move away from more "formal" business communications has occurred as science has revealed that our brains prefer processing knowledge by more narrative means. (A trend toward a more human, authentic style of leadership has also played a role.) Stories are powerful because they provide context that is lacking from abstract prose; they put knowledge into a framework that is more life-like, truer to our day-to-day existence. As such, they can convey insights into norms of behaviour better than almost any other medium.[6] Many well-told stories also often involve something new or unexpected or demonstrate a surprise connection. (To paraphrase John Le Carre, "The cat sat on the mat" is not much of a story but "The cat sat on the dog's mat" suddenly implies interesting possibilities . . .)[7] In doing so, they become an effective way to spark curiosity and insight.

In the context of an experiential learning cycle, stories allow people to share experiences in an effective way, turning an organisation into a social learning unit where new insights are continually available. While a story is not as good as an actual experience, it is the next best thing. The narrative form allows us to be a fly on the wall or have the storyteller's experience in a surrogate fashion. By reading or listening to a story, we can acquire an understanding of a situation's key concepts and their relationships in the same manner as the storyteller.

So creating an environment for stories to be told is a powerful strategy in building a learning culture. The idea is less about making corporate communications narrative based (although that can be effective as well) and more about creating platforms where employees can share stories with each other. Existing internal communications platforms, regular team meetings, and embedded work processes all present opportunities to encourage storytelling and share stories. These tools should be used to encourage personal reflection and the sharing of stories as soon as any meaningful experience has occurred.

Microsoft, for instance, uses a number of tactics to communicate a strong narrative to its stakeholders around the company's brand. These approaches include highlighting stories from CEO Satya Nadella on his LinkedIn account and a stories webpage that looks at news from the angle of how the company's purpose and values come to life. They also have a Story Labs page that features some of Microsoft's newest innovations explained in a compelling story format. The company's Chief Storyteller Steve Clayton is responsible for Microsoft's company storytelling, both internally and externally, with a mission to help the world understand who Microsoft is and the impact its technology and people have on the world.

The perceived wisdom about a "great story" is that it requires meticulous, obsessive preparation to ensure it is fully tailored to a particular audience, delivering the emotional punch and desired insights in exactly the right way. Storytelling in a learning context, however, is different: the key objective is the learning – both for storyteller and the listener – and as such, the stories can be somewhat "raw," at least initially. The act of telling the story should help the storytellers clarify their own insights, as well as spark new insights for the people hearing or reading the story. Constant experimentation with the way someone tells their story also has the benefit of directly triggering the seeking system.

Introduce Pattern Disrupts

As mentioned, in addition to encouraging experiential learning, pattern disrupts – deliberately challenging established and predictable patterns of thought – can create the right conditions for more meaningful insights, more often. Pattern disrupts can be introduced in various ways and they represent powerful strategies for igniting the seeking system at scale. The number of tools and techniques available for pattern disrupts is almost infinite (a brief look at creativity literature will show you), but they can typically be placed into four categories: changing the context, making connections, diving deep, and empathising.

Changing the Context

When we experience any type of challenge at work, the context of the situation will shape how we think about the challenge. Our past experiences, our assumptions about what we could or should do, and any constraints we face (including rules, available resources, systems, or methodologies we are expected to use) all influence the way we think about the problem.

We can disrupt our thought patterns to yield new and fresh insights by holding a "thought experiment" where we pretend that the context has changed. The global research and advisory firm Gartner[8] has found that managers tend to consider "constraints" (part of the context) one of the main obstacles to insight. Whether these constraints are a focus on immediate goals, a lack of resources, or compliance restrictions, common wisdom suggests that by getting rid of rules and boundaries, insight will occur, and creativity and innovative thinking will thrive.

Research by Oguz Acar at Cass Business School,[9] however, challenges this wisdom, suggesting that managers can actually generate better insights by *embracing* constraints. Acar's research reviewed 145 empirical studies and found that individuals, teams, and organisations all benefit from having some constraints in place. It is only when the constraints become too high that they stifle innovation and creativity. In short, constraints force us to think creatively. To develop a solution, therefore, first define, then frame, and finally stretch those constraints temporarily to see if new insights appear. Let's apply this approach to the example of trying to increase the sales performance of your team:

- **Define the constraints**. Start by making explicit the people, time, money, processes, rules, regulations, and cultural norms within which you have to solve your problem. In the case of increasing sales performance, the constraints may include the inability to sell a product until the development team have released it or the inability to increase headcount of the sales team.
- **Frame the constraints as a challenge.** The same constraint may be interpreted in different ways – as a challenge we can handle or as a threatening situation we can't (revisit the "Enablers or Constraints" exercise in Chapter 4 for a refresher). As such, cognitive reframing becomes a critical step when generating fresh insights. Try thinking about the problem in two ways: by framing the constraints as creative challenges, managers can build an understanding of constraints as positives, and thus invite more creativity. By framing the problem as a learning problem, and not as an execution problem, the seeking system is immediately activated and motivation to learn and explore is increased.[10]
- **Stretch the constraints**. Here the idea is to take these constraints and "stretch" them in multiple directions. Initially, make the constraints *harder*. Conduct a thought experiment around solving the problem with 10 percent of the current budget, or in a quarter of the time. These "stretches" can be enough to create that spark of insight. Considering the problem of hitting monthly sales targets, you could stretch the constraint by first posing the question, "What if we had to meet hourly sales targets?" This question could prompt the following chain of thought: "Hourly sales targets; currently each member of the sales team averages ten new sales a week, so that would be 0.25 sales per hour. How can we measure that? Perhaps we should pay more attention to the sales funnel rather than just booked revenue? To make ten sales, team members have to make 40 calls – one per hour. How about setting up a "one-hour challenge" where employees have to contact a client every hour of the working day to encourage more client interaction?"

We are often not conscious of the context in which we operate. By making that context visible, framing it as an exciting challenge, and holding thought experiments that temporarily change the context, we disrupt our thought patterns and give ourselves the opportunity to generate fresh insights that ignite the seeking system.

Making Connections

"Creativity is just connecting things." So observed Steve Jobs in a 1995 interview for *Wired* magazine.[11]

> When you ask creative people how they did something, they feel a little guilty because they didn't really do it, they just saw something. It seemed obvious to them after a while. That's because they were able to connect experiences they've had and synthesise new things. And the reason they were able to do that was that they've had more experiences or they have thought more about their experiences than other people.

So the skill behind creativity is the ability to spot new connections between familiar thoughts.

To make unusual connections, you first need some unusual stimulus to disrupt your thought patterns. You could invite suppliers, clients, or speakers from different fields to address your employees on a regular basis. Or you could temporarily change the environment to set the right conditions. A number of creative exercises exist to try and force a connection between unrelated concepts and spark new insights. One such exercise is called the creative leap.

Exercise: Creative Leap

What Is It?

This exercise can be used in a meeting or workshop to generate new ideas about a topic the team feels stuck on. The creative leap is based on the Edward De-Bono creativity exercise "random word," where people try to identify how a random word relates, or could relate, to a problem statement, in which the issue the team is facing is clearly explained. As this exercise tends to work best when the random word is a noun, a nice way to run the exercise is to ask people to bring a collection of photos and images into the session. They can cut images out of magazines, bring old photos, or print images out from the internet.

How Long Does It Take?

Approximately one hour

Group Size?

Teams of up to eight

How Does It Work?

Step One

Ask each person to bring three to four images with them to the session. Put a large sheet of flip-chart paper on the meeting table, with the problem statement written in the middle (e.g., How to win new customers amid increasing consolidation within our industry?). Place the images face down on the table around the flip-chart paper.

Step Two

Select one image and turn it over. Ask each participant the following question once the image is shown: "How does this image relate to the problem we are facing?" This can be tricky to comprehend at first, so as the leader, you need to move the exercise along with directed, specific questions that will get the participants to open up and really start thinking about the problem in a new way.

For example, say you have an image of a window with some velvet curtains. Ask, "How does this visual relate to the problem of winning new customers?" Have the group consider some of the *characteristics* of the image. Someone might reply, "Well it's a window, so it's transparent. Maybe if we were more transparent about our pricing model, we'd gain more trust and win more customers?"

Catching on, another team member might say, "The curtains slide open and closed. I wonder if we could design a 'price-slider' on our website that could quickly tell customers what products are available in their price range?" Another may build on this idea: "Yes, and the curtains are crushed velvet. How about we introduce a 'price crusher' that not only shows our own products but compares and beats the price of our competitors?"

Other chains of thought can pop up by asking participants about the *emotions* that the image triggers, or what *activities* they perceive when looking at the image. So, people may see a picture of a garden and say, "I look at that and imagine myself at a barbecue, laughing with friends." Now try and relate that new mental image to the problem as before. Keep asking questions to maintain engagement and help the participants come up with their own ideas – don't provide any for them.

Step Three

Once people get the idea of the exercise, turn over each image in turn and engage in this team brainstorming for about five minutes per image. Encourage the team to free-associate, which can generate fresh insights.

Step Four

A collective energy typically forms around the best ideas. As a team, start to make a list of the actions you could take in response to the ideas created. These responses could include testing the feasibility of some promising ideas, further prioritisation, or running a pilot or experiment. Pace is important to igniting seeking system engagement, so ask the team to make specific commitments as to when they will complete the agreed actions, how they will test their effectiveness, and if and when the group could reconvene to review progress.

Diving Deep

Insights can occur if we are willing to stick with a thought or idea longer than we typically might, diving deeper to explore all the nooks and crannies we may have otherwise ignored. Simple "deep dive" exercises can help unlock fresh insights about a problem. For example, there is the "Five Whys" in which you ask why a situation is occurring, then why the answer is occurring, and so on five times until you reach the root cause of the problem. Similarly, exercises that build on others' ideas can take insights to new places as well. One such exercise is called Brainwriting.

Exercise: Brainwriting

What Is It?

Brainwriting is a nonverbal brainstorming method that provides an opportunity for team members to build on each other's ideas, leading to new insights. First credited to German marketing professional Bernd Rohrbach in the late 1960s,[12] Brainwriting can alleviate two of the most common brainstorming pitfalls: unbalanced conversation, in which a few team members dominate the conversation, and the anchoring effect, in which the group formulates a bias in favour of the first idea that comes up during a brainstorming session.[13]

How Long Does It Take?

30–60 minutes

Group Size?

Small teams of up to six people; can be scaled by having lots of small teams work on the same problem

How Does It Work?

Step One

You and your team need to identify the challenge you want to brainstorm. This can be done before the session begins, but also give the team five minutes to discuss the challenge at the beginning of the meeting to make sure you are solving for the right problem.

Step Two

Each person should individually write the creative challenge down at the top of their own large piece of paper and underline it. For example, "How to increase booked sales revenues." Each person then draws a grid on the page with three columns, and as many rows as you have people on the team, as shown in Figure 5.2. From there, participants should spend five minutes writing down three ideas that relate to the challenge in the top row of the grid. The exercise is conducted in silence.

How to increase booked sales revenue

Idea 1	Idea 2	Idea 3
~~ ~~~~~~~	~~~~~~~~~~~	~~~~~~~~~~~ ~~~~~~~~~~~

Figure 5.2

Ideas Template

Step Three

Everyone then passes their sheet of paper to the team member on their right, who will then build off of the three ideas, adding three new thoughts or creative strategies to the paper in the row below. They can build off the ideas above or create new ones. For example, one idea could be "introduce a one-hour sales challenge." When this is passed to the next person, it can be deepened or built on. Someone might write "Create an app to gamify the challenge" or "make real-time data available."

Step Four

Each round lasts five minutes. At the end of each round, have everyone pass the piece of paper to the right again until each template is complete.

This way, with a six-member team, you will have generated 108 ideas in 30 minutes.

Step Five

Once the ideas have made it around the circle, the divergent thinking now requires some convergence on the ideas that the team feels to be most promising. This could be done by "dot voting" (putting all templates on the wall and giving each team member three sticky dots to vote for their favourite ideas), or through "affinity mapping" (asking the group to silently link similar ideas). The group then discusses the individual choices and decides which are the best to pursue as a group. The emerging ideas create a virtuous circle of small intrinsic rewards, releasing dopamine and energising the whole team.

Empathise

Seeing a problem or situation from the point of view of another person is a great way of stimulating new insights. While the premise is simple, this cognitive trick can sometimes be difficult to achieve. To help, try taking a lesson from the social science of ethnography. Ethnography involves embedding oneself deeply in an environment to systematically document the everyday lives, behaviours, and interactions of a community of people. More in depth than simple observation, it requires the researcher to actually participate in the environment they are observing.

Advertising agencies – who rely on being fully tapped into consumer culture to stimulate creative ideas to sell a product or service – often use a form of ethnography when trying to establish what consumers really care about. Saatchi & Saatchi, for example, famously spent days in the homes of new mothers while working on a campaign for Pampers. The resulting insight was that new mothers care more about their babies' development than simply dry diapers, which became the core idea that successfully drove the brand's development for years.

In my consulting work, I always try to "hang out" with clients' employees beyond the confines of an organised workshop. If it's a consumer business I'm working with, I also try and become a customer, ordering the product or spending time at their stores. In my experience this time is *always* well spent. In our never-ending drive for more efficiency, it's easy to dismiss this type of activity as just a "nice to have" but, time and again, this is where breakthrough insights come from.

Ethnography research can be applied to any stakeholder group that you want to understand better: your customers, your employees, your clients, your suppliers. While professional ethnographic researchers can spend months with communities of people, it's possible to apply some of their rigour and intentionality to an activity that may take just a few minutes. This type of empathising can keep new insights flowing. The following are practical ways to implement ethnographic approaches to spark insight:

- **Get into the trenches**. Wharton professor Sigal Barsade recommends that leaders should spend 20 percent of their time doing the work of their subordinates. It's only through experiencing what they experience that you will be able to fully appreciate the challenges they face and develop new insights about what they really care about.
- **Try contextual interviewing**. To increase your understanding of people's behaviours and actions, interviews may be necessary. These should take place in the context of use. For example, if you are interviewing a customer, do so in your store. Interviews should also be conducted immediately after witnessing something that hinted at an insight. In the store example, this could be just after the customer made a purchase.
- **Collect archival data**. Many organisations have other information or physical artifacts that you can use to deepen your understanding and empathy. Review branding, phone conversations, marketing collateral, e-mail, websites, and the physical environment to best connect with the culture of the enterprise.
- **Become your customer.** Buy your product, try your service, and keep a journal of your experiences and reactions. After becoming a customer for a client who specialised in early morning grocery deliveries, for example, my wife and I realised the real benefit of their service. At the time, our four young children all needed packed lunches for school. With my wife and I both trying to get to work, as well as our kids to school, mornings could be *stressful*. And the last thing we needed was to open the fridge and find we had run out of cheese and yogurt to put in the kids' lunch boxes. It was only through living this experience, and then reflecting on it (following the experiential learning cycle described earlier in the chapter), that we came to understand what the grocery delivery service was

actually providing – it was *de-stressing our mornings*. No cheese in the fridge, no problem! Look on the doorstep and we would find a little box of pre-ordered grocery essentials. This insight – that the company's actual job was to make customers' mornings better – helped us to expand the role of the delivery drivers and personalise their purpose. This insight would never have happened without having become a customer.

We often talk about "walking a mile in another's shoes" but typically try and achieve this through the power of imagination alone. It is only by taking the trouble to *experience* the lives of our most important stakeholders that we gain insights that can not only ignite our own seeking systems, but also help us to deepen and develop meaningful relationships with people who are important to us and our organisations.

Summary

- Insight is a moment in time in which you have a deep and sudden real-isation that makes you look at a situation, a problem, yourself, or even the world in a different way. You must create the appropriate conditions for people to have more meaningful insights, more often. To do so at scale, you can encourage experiential learning and introduce pattern disrupts.
- For learning to be effective, the learner must progress through the five stages of the experiential learning cycle. Without reflection, though, insight may not occur, and the learning experience itself may fail.
- To encourage experiential learning within your organisation, sched-ule regular reviews (such as pre-mortems and after action reviews), develop learning goals, and incorporate storytelling internally and externally.
- Our brains rely on predictable patterns of thought through repetition and habit, so we know how to react to stimuli without having to expend too much energy. Insights can occur, however, when we break out of these existing thought patterns.
- To introduce pattern disrupts, reframe boundaries by stretching the con-straints, make connections through unusual stimuli, dive deep using exercises like brainwriting, and empathise with others through ethno-graphic research.

Notes

1   FedEx (1965) "Time Flies – FedEx in Europe Timeline." WWW.fedex.com/en-hu/about/company-info/history.html

2   Kolb, David A. (2014) *Experiential Learning: Experience as the Source of Learning and Development.* Second Edition, Pearson Education, Upper Saddle River, New Jersey.

3   Klein, G. (2007) "Performing a Project Premortem." *Harvard Business Review*, September. Performing a Project Premortem (hbr.org).

4   Mitchell, Deborah J., J. Edward Russo, and Nancy Pennington (1989) "Back to the future: temporal perspective in the explanation of events." *Journal of Behavioral Decision Making* 2, no. 1: 25–38.

5   Morrison, John E., and Larry L. Meliza. Foundations of the after action review process. Institute for Defense Analyses Alexandria Va, 1999.

6   Sole, D. (1995) *Storytelling in Organizations: The Power and Traps of Using Stories to Share Knowledge in Organizations.* LILA Harvard University. Storytelling Brief, v9.PDF (psu.edu).

7   Barber, Michael (1977, September 25) "John le Carré: an interrogation." *New York Times.* https://www.nytimes.com/1977/09/25/archives/john-le-carre-an-interrogation-le-carre.html

8   www.gartner.com/smarterwithgartner/innovate-resource-constrained-environment/

9   Creativity and Innovation Under Constraints: A Cross-Disciplinary Integrative Review Oguz A. Acar, Murat Tarakci, Daan van Knippenberg, October, 2018.

10 Edmondson, A.C., and Z. Lei (2014) "Psychological safety: the history, renaissance, and future of an interpersonal construct." *Annual Review Organizational Psychology and Organizational Behavior* 1, no. 1: 23–43.

11 Wolf, G. (1996) "Steve Jobs: The Next Insanely Great Thing." *Wired*, February 1.

12 Rohrbach, Bernd (1969) "Kreativ nach Regeln – Methode 635, eine neue Technik zum Lösen von Problemen (Creative by rules – Method 635, a new technique for solving problems)." *Absatzwirtschaft* 12: 73–75.

13 Heslin, P. A. (2009) "Better than brainstorming? Potential contextual boundary conditions to brainwriting for idea generation in organizations." *Journal of Occupational and Organizational Psychology* 82(1): 129–145.

6

Leading Through Questions

It was 2010 when Anna Cleland was asked to help with a project to upgrade of the Bank of New Zealand's retail branch network. This was a NZ$220m investment program – no small change for a bank of this size – and the project was not going well. The bank was already two years into the execution phase of a major strategy shift to make the retail branch more customer-focused. The team responsible for the revamp had virtually ground to a halt. Disagreements about the most appropriate design, slow decision making, and missed deadlines had resulted in a dispirited team and concerned senior leadership.

While it may have been tempting to "knock heads together" and elicit fear by talking about the need for everyone to get their act together, Anna took a different approach. She asked questions. Seems simple enough, yes? But as one of the most powerful leadership skills for helping others to achieve insight, it's also one of the most underutilised. When tailored appropriately, questions can ignite the seeking system by helping people form new neural connections and crystalise the type of critical insights discussed in Chapter 5.

Anna started to enquire about the mission the team was on and the outcome they were trying to achieve. She did this both individually and in team meetings, and most often received a response along the lines of "to deliver a quality refurbishment on time and budget." This statement came as no surprise – the team was working to upgrade their retail branches, after all, and like any project, they had deadlines and a budget to work with. Whenever she got an answer, though, she dug a little deeper: "And what is the benefit of that?"

Her team would pause as new neural connections started forming: "Well, a number of things I guess . . . We will have consistent branding across all

DOI: 10.4324/9781003396833-10

our branches." "Branches will be more pleasant for customers." "Working will be more pleasant for employees." With each response, there was room for more exploration. For example, Anna would follow up with, "What is the benefit of a more pleasant environment for customers?"

These questions and answers helped the team realise they were treating the project as a *property refurbishment program*, not a *customer experience program*. By expanding their frame, it became clear how their work could actually help other people – their customers. This realisation proved to be energising, as it helped activate the key seeking system trigger of personalising your purpose. The team was no longer focused on property refurbishment, but on the impact that their work could have on their customers. This insight gave the team a fresh sense of purpose and a clear direction. The spark of ignition had occurred.

Asking the right questions at the right time to ignite the seeking system is a critical leadership skill. It takes practice and experimentation, but it all begins with the right mindset. And when it comes to leading with questions, that means coming from a place of focused curiosity. When I spoke to Sharon Sands, head of leadership assessment, development, and coaching at the advisory firm Heidrick & Struggles, she explained the idea in the context of a "coach and coachee" relationship. "To create insights, both the coach and the coachee must be in a state of quiet awareness," she says. Like focused curiosity, quiet awareness is required to be receptive to insight, as discussed in Part 2. Here, "quiet" refers to a low level of overall activity in our neocortex – a reduced cognitive load and lower threat response. "Awareness" means we are ready to direct our thinking toward subtle internal signals, hunches that we may have about the situation we are reflecting on.

Sands continues,

> It's not just about asking a series of transactional questions. It's about recognizing the unique gifts of your coachee, engaging with them in an adult-to-adult way from a position of curiosity. What's important is paying attention to the subtle nuances of the conversation – that is what will prompt you to ask the right question at the right time.

In short, it's about being *interested*, rather than *interesting*, which contributes to two-way relationships that reinforce themselves. For example, the coach may have insights of their own during the exchange and learn just as much as the coachee. When leaders ask the right questions at the right time, a mutually beneficial interaction takes place, paving the way for individual, team, and eventually organisation-wide ignition.

Asking the Right Questions

Helping people ignite their seeking systems is about creating a mental "gap" in current thought processes and inviting people to fill that gap by making subtle connections of their own. Serving as a call to adventure, a good question can ignite the imagination. The way you initiate an inquiry can inspire the right emotions, cause reflection, and lead to revelations. The best way to find the questions that work for you is to experiment. What follows is a series of 12 questions that I have used extensively in my consulting work and that have helped individuals, teams, and organisations achieve the dopamine rush that ignites our seeking systems.

Whilst not intended to be a formal coaching model or a series of transactional questions, they provide a starting point for leaders to experiment. The questions follow a simple sequence that can unlock potential and possibilities. The sequence starts by helping people gain clarity on what they want to achieve. It then assists them in better understanding their current context before identifying creative ways of reaching those goals. Finally, the sequence aims to convert the initial desire caused by seeking system ignition into commitments for the future. Though the questions are focused on what you as a leader would ask your individual team members, they can also be adapted for use in a group setting.

1. What's Your Mission Right Now?

This question aims to highlight the goal, rather than the problem, just as suggested when building your frame (Chapter 4). Focusing on the goal primes our brains to notice information relevant to the solution. If you were to ask the more ubiquitous, "What is the problem you are trying to solve?" the problem is emphasised, which is more likely to activate the negative emotions associated with the problem itself, narrowing cognition and inhibiting insight. Positive expectations of seeking and finding a solution release more dopamine, increasing the likelihood of ignition and encouraging people to continue working toward the goal.

2. And What Else?

The first answer someone gives to any question is rarely their best, so a great follow-up to the question above (or to any question, actually) is to ask, "And what else?" The question deepens the thoughts and response, increasing the chances of insight. Asking the question also gives leaders more time to slow down and understand the real issue, as compared to rushing to action or immediately giving advice before you know what's really going on.

3. How Would You Tackle the Problem if It Didn't Manifest Until Next Year?

This question utilises a psychological phenomenon called construal level theory, which describes the relationship between *psychological distance* – the degree to which people feel removed from a phenomenon – and the extent to which people's thinking is abstract or concrete. The more distant the phenomenon, the more abstract your thinking will be about the subject; the closer the phenomenon, the more concrete your thinking. Note this distance is not limited to physical distance. It can also be thought of in terms of how socially distant you are from the people involved, how likely you believe the situation is to happen, or how long it will be before the phenomenon is likely to occur. By asking this question about the problem as something happening in the future, you increase the temporal distance, or time, viewing it in a potentially different way as you look at the bigger picture, not just the minute details.

4. When Does the Problem Not Occur?

With its roots in Solution-Based Therapy and Appreciative Inquiry, this question – often called the "exception question" – subtly demonstrates that not only are we capable of solving our own problems, but that in some way we have *already solved them*, at least in some circumstances. Say two teams at your company regularly feud over the amount of work one team creates for the other. By asking them, "When does this not occur?" you highlight times when the teams have either been in alignment or have successfully collaborated. In doing so, you may uncover specific examples that can be analysed and point to a solution that has already proven to be workable. Asking about exceptions then leads to better understanding and positive results.

5. How Would You Persuade Someone like Yourself That This Situation is Positive?

This question helps people to reframe their current context if having a negative view of their circumstances is holding them back. It involves the use of a psychological principle called self-persuasion, meaning it places people in a situation where they are effectively motivated to persuade themselves to change their own attitudes or behaviour. You might ask a project manager, "How would you persuade a group of project managers that using this new IT system was a good thing?" In thinking about and answering this question, the project manager is effectively coming up with an answer to persuade him or herself. By offering their own answer, they are more likely to believe and act upon it.

6. Is There Anything Else I Should Have Asked That I Didn't?

This question always provides further insight. It is similar to "And what else?" and it gives people an opportunity to identify those elements of their current situation that they initially felt uncomfortable raising. The people who you work with, and especially who work for you, may be waiting to be asked about a number of issues to explain current pain points, ideas, or even good news, but if they aren't given the opportunity, they may never speak up.

7. What Intuitions Do You Have About a Solution?

This question is especially useful for brainstorming solutions at work. Not only can you use it to prompt ignition in others, but also in yourself. For many of us, a thought doesn't seem "real" unless we say it out loud and get it into discussion as a way to road test it. As neuroscientists John Kounios and Mark Beeman point out, "Intuitions are examples of a type of mental process that is neither fully conscious nor unconscious."[1] Intuitions can herald insights by helping us make subtle connections. This question encourages attention on those subtle connections by simply asking about them. Instead of getting saddled with the need to go through a long narrative of why a solution is good or bad, this question allows individuals to openly verbalise and study any ripple of an idea in their subconscious, which can lead to a fruitful discussion about possible solutions.

8. If You Woke Up in the Morning and the Problem Was Solved, What Would Be the First Small Sign That Things have Changed?

Sometimes called "the miracle question," and derived from solutions-based therapy, this question is meant to help people identify concrete and tangible signs that the "miracle" has happened, rather than describing the miracle itself. As a leader, you may have to prod team members for specifics. For example, if a team member came to you feeling stressed by an excessive workload, you may have the following dialogue:

You:	Imagine while you're sleeping tonight, a miracle happens and all the troubles that brought you here are resolved. When you wake up in the morning, what's the first small sign you'd see that would make you think the problem has gone?
Team member:	Rather than feeling my anxiety rising, I'd feel at ease. In control instead of out of control. I'd get ready for work feeling excited for the day ahead.
You:	What would you do when you got to work?
Team member:	Well, first up, my desk would be tidy, not covered in papers. I would have a clear plan for the day's work, and would have scheduled important, but not urgent, tasks for when I'm feeling my most energised, which, for me, is in the morning.
You:	How would you react to distractions, such as phone calls or e-mails, as they arise?
Team member:	I wouldn't be reacting to such distractions because I would have disabled my email and phone while I'm doing a block of important work.
You:	What's to stop you doing that now?

Notice the part of the question that asks about *the first small sign*. This is important because you want to avoid people talking about unattainable miracles, such as "a kind colleague would have taken all my work away from me and everything would be fine," or something else that would be totally unfeasible in reality. The concrete specifics further enable people to envisage a future state that is truly achievable.

9. What Would the Greatest Leader You've Ever Had Do Now?

Another common but powerful coaching question, this one enables people to remove themselves from the constraints of their own personality and ego, looking at the challenge from a different perspective. By asking, "What would Steve Jobs do?" for example, it can break people out of established patterns of thought and create fresh insights about any challenge. It is an extremely effective question in gaining a breakthrough insight to a problem where an impasse has been reached.

10. What Needs to Be Done Tomorrow at 8:35 AM?

This question allows people to think more concretely and specifically, focusing on a topic when it is in close psychological proximity. In construal level theory, this question has what is known as low-level construal. When people are engaged in low-level construal, they focus on the present in great detail, allowing them to take the necessary actions to get started and make progress. The question ties conceptual ideas and discussion to real-world action that actually needs to be carried out. Being specific about a time and date also utilises the "pique technique,"[2] whereby people are more likely to comply with requests that are unusually specific, because it piques their interest and helps ignite the seeking system.

11. How Would You Model the Required Personal Changes You Are Asking of the Organisation?

This question is really more for you than your team members. When an organisation transforms, its leaders must take action that demonstrates the behaviour change required of the whole team or organisation. Personal change cannot be sidestepped and this question can result in new specific behaviours you can practice that will symbolise the transformation and make it tangible for others.

12. What Would Happen if You Did Nothing?

This simple question can be a catalyst for moving people into a conversation about the different possibilities for change. The juxtaposition of comparing the status quo with an exciting future can help people look at the personal consequences of inaction and inspire them to action. The question often prompts a kind of "jolt" from the recipient and can be followed up with a question like, "So what will you do now?"

Engaging Groups With Questions

While questions used to ignite the seeking system in individuals can also be applied effectively to teams, a slightly different dynamic is in play. Leaders need to find ways to help a team collectively reach insights, co-create, allow everybody a voice, and build on each other's ideas. To get there, there are a number of question-based methodologies and exercises you can use to ignite the seeking systems of both small and large groups.

Appreciative Inquiry

Appreciative inquiry is a question-based, group methodology designed to find the best in people and their organisations. Originally proposed in an article by David Cooperrider and Suresh Srivastva,[3] it involves systematic discovery of what gives "life" to an organisation when it is most effective and capable in economic, ecological, and human terms. Appreciative inquiry assumes that every organisation has a positive core and that discovering this core can provide inspiring new insights able to ignite the seeking systems of whole groups. Changes never thought possible can be suddenly and democratically mobilised.

By focusing on the positive core – and appreciating and valuing the best of what already exists in the organisation – seeking systems are ignited without the threat response that can come from the problem-solving paradigm typically employed in a work setting. Problems are not ignored in appreciative inquiry, they are simply validated and then reframed. For example, a problem of how to fix low management credibility (which can trigger defensiveness) becomes an inquiry into how to amplify existing moments of inspired leadership (which triggers the seeking system). Both address the issue but approach it from a different perspective. By investing in what already works in human and organisation systems, appreciative inquiry shortens the path to achieving organisational success.

This methodology is often used as a basis for major changes in an organisation. While there is no strict formula for appreciative inquiry, most change efforts flow through the following cycle:

Step One: Define. In this step, the group decides on the topic that will be the focus of the inquiry. The topic can be anything of strategic importance to the group or organisation. It may be to reduce costs, improve quality, speed up new product cycle time, create cultural change, or instigate an organisational turnaround. Whatever the topic, it must be *positively framed*, rather than negatively. So "cutting R&D costs" becomes an inquiry into "developing frugal innovation"; "reducing product defects" becomes "replicating the perfect product." Once defined, the remaining steps are often run through in what is known as an AI summit. These may take up to three to four months to plan, three to four days to conduct, and three to four months to follow up, depending on their size. AI summits range from 30 to 3,000 people. The closer they get to including every member of the system, the more dramatic and sustainable the impact.

Step Two: Discovery. Day one of a typical summit involves discovering and connecting the many facets of what is known as the organisation's "positive core." These include the strengths, assets, competencies, capabilities, values, traditions, and rituals that fuel and sustain success. Appreciating the best of "what is" emphasises the art of crafting positive questions. Small teams explore questions like:

- When have you felt most alive and effective in your work life?
- What do you value most about what you do at work, and the impact the organisation has?
- What makes this organisation feel like a great place to work? What are the key factors that make this possible?

At the end of the day, a deep understanding of the "positive core" will have been developed by everyone at the summit.

Step Three: Dream. Day two of the summit often includes envisioning the organisation's future in bold and specific terms. The group use the positive core to inform the process. Together, they create and share images

109

and co-create possibilities of what an exciting future might look, sound, and feel like when the "positive core" comes to life.

Step Four: Design. Day three includes working backwards from the dream, defining the steps needed to achieve it. This may include necessary changes to strategies, structures, systems, and processes within the organisation.

Step Five: Destiny. The final day is all about planning for action. Individual commitments are made, cross-functional initiatives launched, and alignment formed through a large group dialogue. The summit close becomes the launch of the change program – one in which the seeking systems of the whole group have been ignited.

Organisations such as John Deere, McDonalds, the U.S. Navy, and countless others have used AI summits to engage their whole organisations through the art of asking unconditional, positive questions. In doing so they have ignited the seeking systems of thousands of employees.

World Café

What Is It?

The World Café enables leaders to create open and generative conversations about the questions that are critical to the real work of the organisation. This conversational process, through which participants co-create their collective futures, is an approach for engaging people in a conversation about a key operational or strategic issue. The World Café not only taps into the collective creative intelligence of a large group, but also engages the seeking system at scale. The final aim is to engage a whole system of people in creating their own high-performance future.

How Long Does It Take?

The whole process can be done in as little as two hours, but more in-depth exploration may take up to several days.

Group Size?

From 12 to 1,000 people

How Does it Work?

Step One

Though a World Café is not facilitated in the traditional sense, a master of ceremonies introduces a question (chosen and framed in a similar manner to step
1 of the appreciative inquiry process) and coordinates the various conversation
rounds in the following steps. The group is split into small clusters of four to
five people who, traditionally, sit around a café-style table together. A world-
café with a group of 30 may therefore be set up as six café-style tables in a
large room with five people sitting at each table (or, if being done remotely, in
six virtual breakout rooms). Each group is invited to explore the same or similar questions, which should be important to the participants' work.

Step Two

The opening round of conversation takes 20–30 minutes. Participants at each
table take notes on the discussion, highlighting key points they found useful.
Sometimes paper tablecloths are laid on the café tables for this purpose.

Step Three

At the end of this first round, participants are invited to change tables and
carry key ideas and insights from their previous conversation into a newly
formed group. (Feel free to have them do so in an unstructured way or assign
them to tables to ensure different participants interact throughout the exercise.) Each table has a "host" who remains at the table throughout the event
and shares the key insights from prior dialogues with the new arrivals. The
event consists of several – typically three – rounds of conversation. This
cross-pollination of ideas is one of the hallmarks of the World Café.

Step Four

After completing the rounds of conversation, the table hosts harvest recur-
ring points from the dialogues and share them with all participants. The
World Café creates generative networks of conversation based on important
questions. The approach allows participants to access mutual intelligence in
service of a common goal. In doing so, seeking systems are not only ignited
at scale, but a vehicle is provided to build trust, nurture relationships, and
create new possibilities for action.

Exercise: Fishbowl Discussion

What Is It?

The fishbowl discussion works as a forum to address some of the toughest questions teams need to ask about themselves. This discussion is used to re-frame thinking and provide clarity on how to move forward. Rather than a large group having an open discussion about a problem – which can be difficult to mediate and often only benefits a few active participants – a smaller group is isolated to discuss the issue at hand. The rest of the participants sit in a circle around the smaller group and observe without interrupting. Fishbowls can be particularly effective when questions need to be asked and insights need to be uncovered about team dynamics or any group tensions that may exist. Facilitation is focused on the core group discussion. The fishbowl process usually has a facilitator or moderator.

How Long Does It Take?

30 minutes – 2 hours

Group Size?

Typically small, intact teams of up to 12 people, but can work with up to 50 people.

Step One

Agree what question would be useful for the group to explore in order to solve a current problem or achieve a desired goal. For example, this could be, "How do we improve collaboration between team members?"

Step Two

Place two to five chairs in the centre circle and up to 10, or more, chairs on the outside of the circle (dependent on group size), leaving one or two extra chairs both within the circle and without.

Step Three

Invite people to sit in the centre circle and begin a discussion answering the set questions. Only those in the centre circle are allowed to talk. People can join the discussion at any point by sitting in the centre circle in an open chair. If there is no free chair, participants from the outer circle can tap someone on the shoulder; whoever is tapped must leave the centre circle.

Step Four

The facilitator observes from the outside and can also join the centre circle at any point, also by tapping on people's shoulders if no chairs are free. In this way they can share their observations of how the team is handling the discussion.

Step Five

All participants, along with the facilitator, are encouraged to ensure that any topic being purposefully avoided is brought into the circle. They may ask:

- "What is not being said that needs to be said?"
- "What's getting in the way of us learning together?"
- "How do we need to be different to engage with the wider team?"

Step Six

After the conversation concludes, the facilitator debriefs the session by getting feedback from both the inner and outer circles. The magic of this process lies in the personal reflection of each attendee. Participants and observers are enabled to leave the exercise with a greater understanding of the range of opinions that exists within their community. The process also helps a group feel that their views have been represented in a discussion, even if they themselves have not had any direct input. Typically, the transparency of the process and the difficult questions asked builds trust among participants. The exercise also ignites the group's seeking systems as members have new insights and converge on a set of agreed actions.

Creating a Culture of Questions

Perhaps nothing is more important to igniting the seeking system at scale than creating a culture where *everyone* throughout the organisation learns to ask good questions and is willing to participate in active conversations around them. As shown, questions ignite people's passions and energy, creating insights in a way few other techniques can. Since that's the case, one of the most important leadership roles is to build a culture of curiosity, in which all employees, from the C-suite to the front line, ask questions that will ignite seeking systems at scale.

To encourage your whole organisation to do so, you need a way to develop leaders' skills toward that end. Avanade's Dave Gartenberg faced this exact challenge at the 30,000 employee, Seattle-based consulting firm, the world's largest community of experts in Microsoft-based solutions. As CHRO and, more recently, executive in charge of the Transformation Office, Dave is passionate about bringing the best out of all Avanade employees. That's why, upon joining the firm in 2017, the company metrics concerned him. Avanade had what Dave calls a "Watermelon scorecard": green on the outside (excellent financial results) and red on the inside (poor engagement and high employee attrition).

The company needed a refreshed strategy, and new CEO Pamela Maynard spearheaded a transformation effort with a series of design-led sessions meant to illicit ideas about how the firm were to achieve their "unfair" share of market growth. These crowdsourced, question-based sessions (similar to the AI summit described earlier) identified 20 initiatives that would either help the company to sell more of their services or help employees have a better experience.

One of these initiatives was called "Culture for Growth," which included helping the whole organisation to ask better questions, to focus effort on development and personal growth. As CHRO, Dave utilised the levers available to him and embarked on a year-long re-design process of the company Performance Management approach. (Details of how to design such an approach that can ignite, rather than dampen, the seeking system are discussed in Chapter 10.) Key to its success was the introduction of real-time, regular coaching and development conversations between manager and employee. This strategy is heavily dependent on "people managers" who have the skills and motivation to hold these conversations on a regular basis. To ensure that Avanade identified and developed the best people managers, Dave took the following approach:

1. **Start at the top.** Top leaders undertook training on asking effective questions and also role-modelled the habit. They did this not just by asking better questions of others, but by explicitly asking for feedback from the rest of the company. So now, during a typical 60-minute session with

each business unit about the company transformation, Dave devotes 45 minutes to questions by asking, "What questions and feedback do you have for me?"

2. **Assessment & Selection.** In a consulting business such as Avanade, being a career coach or people manager is a critical role typically "inherited" as you became more senior in the company (which it was historically possible to do without having much skill as a people manager, as long as you could sell and deliver work effectively). Dave started assessing people for the role, rather than it just being handed to you as an additional responsibility. This not only helped to ensure that the best people became people managers but also increased the desirability of the role. This applied to both external hires and internal selection.

3. **Training.** People managers were given specific training on how to ask the right questions and have the right type of conversations that would ignite the seeking system, helping their people be the best they could be.

4. **Consequence.** Being a good people manager no longer just got you a pat on the back but could also get you promoted. Dave increased the weighting assigned to being a good coach in the assessment of year-end ratings and promotion.

While Avanade are still on their journey, it is clear they have started to normalise working practices where questions are commonly used – in team meetings as well as in regular coaching conversations – to help employees create their own insights and ignite their seeking systems.

Summary

- Leaders can create insight through questions – and questions-based exercises and methodologies – to ignite their team members' seeking systems.
- Though there are many questions that can result in insight, there are four main categories leaders can focus on. These are questions to: find the goal, understand the current state, find a solution, and encourage action.
- The question-based, group methodology appreciative inquiry can help teams discover what gives "life" to an organisation when it is most effective and capable. By focusing on an organisation's positive core,

employees' seeking systems are ignited without the threat response that can come from the problem-solving paradigm.

- Exercises such as the World Café and the Fishbowl provide a safe, fun environment for employees to explore questions that could be critical to solving problems, achieving a desired goal, or coming up with new approaches to old problems.
- To create a culture of asking questions, it's important to support and develop leadership skills around asking better questions and explicitly seeking out feedback.

Notes

1 Kounios, J., and M. Beeman (2015) *The Eureka Factor: Aha Moments, Creative Insight, and the Brain*. London: Windmill Books, p. 133.

2 Santos, Michael D., Craig Leve, and Anthony R. Pratkanis (1994) "Hey buddy, can you spare seventeen cents? Mindful persuasion and the pique technique." *Journal of Applied Social Psychology* 24, no. 9: 755–764.

3 Cooperrider, D.L., and S. Srivastva (1987) "Appreciative inquiry in organizational life". In Woodman, R.W., and W.A. Pasmore (eds) *Research in Organizational Change and Development* (Vol. 1). Stamford, CT: JAI Press, pp. 129–169.

Activating Organisational Purpose

In the last few years, the idea that a company should stand for something bigger than profit has become central to the public dialogue. Companies have been, and continue to be, on a journey to both understand and connect their stakeholders to a higher-order purpose, in a way that adds value to the enterprise. The hard part – the real test of an organisation's purpose – is figuring out how to make it more than just words on a poster. For purpose to really matter, it needs to go beyond an initiative that sits on the margins of the organisation and be lived and breathed by all stakeholders.

The actions companies take or don't take have become a major factor in their abilities to preserve the trust of their stakeholders, including their valued employees. And companies that put purpose at the core of their strategy are often rewarded through significantly outperforming their competitors. In fact, authors Raj Sisodia, David Wolfe, and Jag Sheth demonstrate in their book, *Firms of Endearment: How World-Class Companies Profit from Passion and Purpose*, how companies driven by purpose outperformed the S&P 500 by 14 times, and Good to Great companies by six times, over a period of 15 years.

Take Unilever, the British multinational consumer goods company. Their purpose is to "make sustainable living commonplace." The companies sustainable living brands are growing 50% faster than the company's other brands and delivering more than 60% of the company's growth[1].

Similarly, during her tenure as the CEO of PepsiCo, Indra Nooyi built a sustainability focus through the Performance with Purpose initiative (PwP). PwP balances superior financial returns with healthier products, less environmental impact, and new types of support for women and families, both

DOI: 10.4324/9781003396833-11

within the Pepsi organisation and in local communities within which they operate. The net revenue over the years after PwP was implemented grew by 80 percent and PepsiCo outperformed both S&P 500 and the Consumer Staples Select index between 2009 and 2019[2].

Companies like Unilever and PepsiCo aspire to live their purpose every day. Their leaders, employees, and stakeholders know what their companies stand for and what they're looking to achieve, aside from an improved bottom line. To reach this point, however, it's not enough to simply "have" an organisational purpose – it must be *activated*.

Just having an organisational purpose often fails to ignite the seeking system because leaders resort to a simple narrative and platitudes around purpose that are disconnected from their employees' actual emotional desires, hopes, or dreams. Purpose is personal and emotional, and it can't just be handed out like playing cards. To help employees feel more purposeful, and ignite their seeking systems in turn, they need to be guided through an *activation journey*. That journey has three steps: allow deep reflection, encourage job-crafting, and highlight the impact of people's work. As leaders, you can use these approaches both for your own understanding and with your teams to make purpose come to life, integrating the three seeking system triggers and igniting the sequence.

Step One: Allow Deep Reflection

When designing an organisational purpose, leadership teams often gather together away from the office for a few days. Usually helped by consultants, these leaders then engage in deeply reflective work together to discuss and crystalise what the company stands for, where it should be heading, and what they want their legacy to be. They may even have profound insights about the company's future and their role within it. These retreats can be quite successful, igniting leaders' seeking systems through the reset, ignite, fuel sequence. Leaders leave feeling energised and excited, and when they return to the office, they can't wait to communicate the new organisational purpose and direction they have agreed upon.

Unfortunately, some tend to forget the process of discovery that brought them to the point of seeking system ignition. They weren't "told" what their personal purpose was, nor were they handed an organisational one. They went through a true process, one that will be required for all employees.

That starts by deepening employee understanding of their strengths, their individual passions, and the organisational purpose – exercises that have an immediate positive benefit.

Janine Dutcher, a psychology professor at UCLA, researches how "positive interventions and experiences may lead to reductions in threat and stress responding." In one experiment, she hooked people up to fMRIs to measure their brain activity as they considered different tasks and ideas. She had half of the subjects write about an everyday item, like a toaster, while she asked the other half to write about their unique values. The fMRIs showed that as people reflected on their unique values, dopamine was released, triggering their seeking systems. There was no such effect when writing about toasters. The study found that when we reflect on our core values, unique passions, and signature strengths (who we are and how we behave when we are at our best), we become energised.[3] Using our strengths and activating our motivations in service of our organisational strategy is the sweet spot that helps us to feel purposeful at work, as shown in Figure 7.1.

So to start the purpose activation journey, allow deep reflection about individual strengths, individual motivations, and organisational purpose. Here's how.

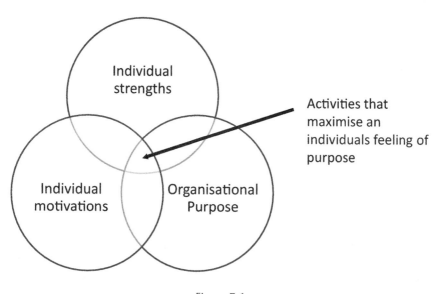

Figure 7.1

Finding the Fit: Reflecting on Strengths, Motivations, and Organisational Purpose

Understand Your Best Self

To gain real-world insights about personal strengths that really pack a punch, it's best to use narrative-based assessments. This means collecting stories from people close to you – friends, family, and past and present colleagues – about times when you have been at your best. Pioneered by Jane Dutton and her colleagues at the University of Michigan, Laura Morgan Roberts at Harvard, and more recently by Dan Cable at London Business School, the approach allows you to build your own "highlights" reel of your most exceptional moments.

Exercise: Highlights Reel

What Is It?

An opportunity to gain insight into how others view the participants, helping them to identify their unique gifts and strengths. By having people describe a specific time in which participants contributed something important to an endeavour, they will better understand their unique qualities to which they can further play.

How Long Does It Take?

Three to five weeks to nominate people in participants' social network and have them write stories about when the participants are, or have been, at their best.

Group Size?

In the context of purpose activation, the highlights reel is best conducted with an intact team of between eight and 25 people. (While understanding one's strengths is beneficial to individual performance, empirical studies show that sharing those strengths with a team also improves team dynamics, including trust, learning capabilities, and performance.)

How Does It Work?

Step One

Have participants think of ten to 20 people who they can nominate as storytellers. These people should be an important part of their lives:

friends, family, mentors, significant others, colleagues, or anyone else who knows them well. The goal is to find a good mix of people whom they would like to thank and learn from. Next, have participants email or speak to each nominated storyteller, asking them to share up to three stories (written, video, or audio) about when the participants have been at their best. Each story should have a beginning (the setting), a middle (what they did), and an end (their impact). The storytellers should include the gritty, specific elements of the event they remember – who was there, what the environment was like, how people were feeling. In addition to collecting stories from others, have participants write two or three stories themselves. These represent their own memories of when they have been at their best.

This part of the exercise may sound daunting, as people often feel awkward asking those close to them to provide this type of positive feedback. But once participants get over the initial discomfort, both they and the storytellers typically find the experience uplifting. Online tools are also available to help collect the stories, which makes the whole process much easier. (For example, the Reflected Best Self Exercise™, that originated from the University of Michigan (https://reflectedbestselfexercise.com/), and the Point Positive tool from Essentic, a company originally founded by Dan Cable of London Business School (https://essentic.com/), are both useful.)

Step Two

All stories should be compiled in one place – this compilation will become the highlights reel – and only read once they have all been received, or on a pre-determined date. One of the online tools mentioned can be used to send highlights reels to all team members 24 hours before a debrief session. Many participants find reading their stories a deeply emotional experience, which can act as a true catalyst for change. The "positive trauma" caused by engaging with your highlights reel creates openness to new ideas, new projects or endeavours, and new possibilities for the future.

Step Three

Have participants read each story and try to remember, and re-experience, these moments when they were at their very best. They should analyse each story by asking themselves what they were thinking, feeling, saying, and doing at the time.

- What were the conditions that led to your actions?
- What were some of the things that you did (or did not) do?
- What strengths did you apply?
- What are the stand-out strengths from your story?

Then, have them read through each analysis and pull out common themes about their strengths. Finally, using prose and not bullet points, have them write a two- to four-paragraph narrative description of their best self. Once all participants have written the narrative description, have them share it with the group. The narrative description is the culmination of the exercise and acts as a powerful summary of all the participants' stories to better recognise their strengths.

Explore Your Personal Purpose

Understanding our best selves is just one part of better understanding our identity. Another is to explore our calling in life – our personal purpose. The idea of having a personal purpose may sound just too "touchy feely" for some but, as shown, connecting with your most important values and motivations is a powerful strategy in igniting the seeking system.

Harvard Researchers Todd Rose and Ogi Ogas have studied individuals who identify as successful by their own measure, which is not always money, status, or power. They found that these people – whom they called Dark Horses – found success and happiness through the relentless pursuit of *fulfilment*. It is commonly assumed that obtaining mastery and success in a chosen field will bring fulfilment, but Rose and Ogas found it was actually the other way around – the act of seeking fulfilment makes people good at what they do and brings them success.[4] So how does one seek fulfilment? Building on Rose & Ogas' work, one way is to identify the things that deeply motivate you *and you want to build your identity around* – your identity motivations.

Exercise: Identity Motivations

What Is It?

Identity motivations are the core and specific *reasons why* you love doing certain activities. They are unique to you, and if you can build your identity around them, and make decisions about how to pursue them, you will unlock greater fulfilment in your life and work, whilst getting closer to living your personal purpose. This exercise helps uncover participants' identity motivations. As the team or group leader, you should also partake in the exercise.

How Long Does It Take?

One hour of pre-work, plus a three-hour workshop.

Group Size?

An individual exercise, but often applied to a group of up to 25 as part of a wider purpose activation journey

How Does It Work?

Step One

Have participants identify three events or activities that they really love. This could be work-related (organising others; the study of human behaviour), a regular activity (having adventures in nature; reading), or a one-off event that was deeply fulfilling (the time I built a tree-house). If you struggle to think of anything, try these prompts:

- If I could talk about something all day long, what would it be?
- What do I seek out, or keep coming back to?
- What do I do just for the sake of doing it?

Step Two

Now have participants privately ask themselves *why* they loved those activities. Let's say that one of the activities you love is rock-climbing. You could conclude that one of your identity motivations is climbing, but that would be a mistake. Instead, ask yourself *why* you like climbing. Maybe you like the feeling of testing yourself or being outside in nature. Or you might find a deep feeling of camaraderie and trust forged by having a challenging shared experience. There's also the feeling of achievement you have when overcoming a difficult challenge.

This deeper reflection is necessary because we tend to base our identity on the things we do, so by understanding *why* we like doing them, we can instead build our identities around these deeper motivations. If you relentlessly pursue climbing as a motivator and part of your identity, but you then get hurt and can't climb, you suddenly lose your identity and opportunity for fulfilment. If you realise you love climbing because it connects you to nature whilst working in a small trusting team, there are literally hundreds of paths you could follow to do just that, outside of climbing. The same applies in a work context. You could build your motivation and identity around becoming CEO. If that doesn't happen (or, sometimes, even if it does) you feel disappointed. Building your identity around specific identity motivations such as a love of learning or creating new service offerings, however, provides an infinite number of possible role options.

Step Three

Test the motivations you have identified by turning them into statements of identity. Let's say that, through the previous steps, you identified the following specific motivations as being most important to you:

1. Learning new skills
2. Doing things that few others ever have
3. Planning and leading adventures
4. Applying multiple skills to a task

Now turn them into identity statements to see if they still resonate:

1. I am a lifelong learner
2. I am an explorer of new ideas and places
3. I am a risk mitigator who likes risk
4. I choose opportunities that use all my skills

Do these statements still resonate? Many people find they want to re-visit their specific motivations after reflecting on their identity (I like playing golf but I'm definitely not a golfer!). Iterate until you find four-to-five statements of identity that resonate.

Step 4

Now activate your personal purpose by choosing behaviours that reflect your identity. So, using the identity statements above, make some behavioural commitments:

1. I will set myself learning goals before every project
2. I will seek to try something new in any project
3. I will choose to explore the risky option as long as I can find ways of mitigating the risk
4. I will intentionally review "fit" with all my strengths and skills before making a choice

Step 5

In this step, participants move beyond internal reflection and share their identity motivations with the group. While identity motivations are deeply individual, creating a forum where team members can discuss them has multiple benefits. First, discussing motivations with close colleagues can help to develop and validate participants thinking as they start to build their personal purpose. Second, the vulnerability shown when sharing these thoughts helps to build trust and improves team dynamics. Third, finding common threads between team members with other similar identity motivations helps to create collective identity.

Reflect on Your Organisational Purpose

Purpose isn't static; its meaning must continue to evolve along with the organisation and the wider environment. For example, a merger or acquisition might require the creation of a whole new purpose as companies combine their histories and create new strategic goals. Whether you are happy with your company's current organisational purpose or whether you believe a refresh is required, employees must be given an opportunity to deepen their understanding about the organisation and what it stands for.

I was lucky enough to work closely with Richard Hytner when he was the world-wide deputy chairman of advertising agency Saatchi & Saatchi.

Richard and his team taught me the power of reframing in order to uncover imaginative or creative insights to common questions. This exercise, designed to help people reflect on organisational purpose, is inspired by that thinking.

Exercise: The *"Really"* Reframe

To help organisations better understand their purposes, it helps to start with a working definition of what it takes to *feel purposeful*. Feeling purposeful goes beyond simply understanding the "why" of the organisation. It also requires that you are intentionally using your strengths in service of helping others. That is, you understand your gifts and how to apply them to have the most positive impact on the world. This leads to a set of questions that, when carefully considered, can generate fresh insights about your business and organisational purpose.

- Who must we help for us to achieve results?
- What do these customers care about?
- What job do we do for these customers?
- What are we good at?
- Who do we compete with?
- What else could we do for our customers?

Allowing yourself time as a team to consider and answer the questions in a meaningful and inspiring way can ignite the seeking systems of the whole team. This requires answering each of the questions twice.

Begin by gathering the team together and have them answer each of the questions in a *literal* way. As you ask each question, write down the responses, then come to a consensus among the group. In the example below, I use the example of a food delivery business, specialising in delivering dairy products and other essentials to customers in the mornings:

- Who must we help for us to achieve results?
  Our doorstep delivery customers
- What do these customers care about?
  Receiving their delivery, on time, in full, every time
- What job do we do for these customers?
  We deliver fresh milk and other products straight to their doors every morning

- What are we good at?
  Logistics – delivering orders on time, in full, in an efficient manner
- Who do we compete with?
  Other food delivery services; the local convenience store
- What else could we do for our customers?
  Increase our product range to compete with other food delivery services

Now – and this is where the magic lies – have the participants answer the questions again, but this time thinking about them on a deeper, more focused, creative, and aspirational level by adding the prefix *"really"* to the questions:

- Who must we *really* help for us to achieve results?
  Those who are time-poor and who value convenience and quality over price (insight: time-poor and affluent often equates to middle-class with young children – should this be our core target market?)
- What do these customers *really* care about?
  They don't want to ever worry about boring but essential chores (insight: ensuring they never run out of essential products is critical. Imagine not having to pack a lunch for your child on a school day when you're trying to get to the office for a meeting.)
- What job do we *really* do for these customers?
  We de-stress their mornings. (insight: by ensuring our customers have what they need every morning we are making their mornings better!)
- What are we *really* good at?
  Doing what we promise for the customer – whatever it takes (insight: our strength in logistics means we always go the extra mile to deliver on our promises. This is an important value for us)
- Who do we *really* compete with?
  The "auto-order" function on Amazon and similar platforms; anyone who brings a little more joy/less stress to an average morning
- What else could we do for our customers?
  We could stretch our product offering to appeal to this purpose of making our customers' mornings better. Dry cleaning? Fresh pastries?

Answering the questions from this "reframe" perspective requires you and your team to put yourselves in your customers' shoes to create emotional insight. As management guru Peter Drucker once said, "The customer rarely buys what the business thinks it sells him." If you have already spent time with your customers to experience your company as they do (as described in Chapter 5), then you should get great answers to these questions during the workshop. Otherwise, the exercise may run over a longer period as you gather the insights needed by spending time with your customers.

When a company's higher purpose is "improving the world,"[5] it can feel abstract or directionless. Running through this exercise with teams can help people connect with purpose in a deeper way. Lego, for example, proclaims it wants to "inspire and develop the builders of tomorrow," rather than sell plastic bricks. Starbucks says it wants "to inspire and nurture the human spirit – one person, one cup and one neighborhood at a time," rather than sell coffee. The Really Reframe helps employees to understand why.

Armed with a deeper understanding of their strengths, passions, and organisational purpose, it's now time for employees to make actual changes to how they work – changes that will ignite their seeking systems and improve their performance. It's time for them to job craft.

Step Two: Encourage Job Crafting

During an interview with leadership advisory firm Heidrick & Struggles in 2020, Liv Garfield, CEO of the British-based water company Severn Trent, said, "Although I can't love every part of my job, I can organise my time so that I love every day. This has been a game changer; it's allowed me to sustain my energy and enthusiasm and be more impactful." Garfield was talking about *job crafting*, the ability to proactively shape your own work environment such that it fits your individual needs, as well as those of your team and organisation.

Now, job-crafting may have been a game changer for Garfield, but she's the CEO – she has the autonomy to make those types of changes. Often, leaders fear that if everyone is given such autonomy, a tradeoff would take place between individual satisfaction and overall efficiency. Their own narrative goes something like this: "Should I just let everyone do what they want and forget about what the organisation and its stakeholders need? And if I let one person do it, do I have to let everyone?" Understandably, people in such positions worry that by letting their team members cherry pick from the work they most enjoy, critical work that may not be desirable or align with an employee's strengths won't get done. This is why job-crafting must be done *in service* of organisational purpose – it provides the framework within which we can all do our best work.

Scientific evidence supports the organisational and individual bene-fits of crafting jobs to fit our purpose, values, and strengths. Research by Amy Wrzesniewski, a professor at Yale School of Management, showed that employees in a Fortune 500 tech company who participated in a job-crafting workshop were significantly happier and more effective in their jobs six weeks later, based on ratings of their colleagues and managers.[6] In another study, Carrie Leana, at the University of Pittsburgh, studied 232 teachers at 62 childcare centres, finding that teachers who crafted their jobs in collaboration with coworkers demonstrated higher performance, particu-larly for less experienced teachers. Collaborative job crafters also were more satisfied with their work and committed to their schools.[7]

So, rather than thinking of work as a rigid structure you and your team must conform to, it is more useful to consider it a flexible system that needs to be crafted and personalised. Once you understand your gifts, your moti-vations, and your company's purpose, you can begin to craft your work around them, further energising you and leading to your best work. And the good news is that you don't have to do this ALL the time. For the benefits of job crafting to really kick in, there is evidence to suggest you and your employees should be aiming to do something they love every day,[8] and for a total of at least 20% of their time.[9] An eminently achievable goal. The fol-lowing exercises will help you and your employees move in that direction.

Exercise: Individual Job Crafting

What Is It?

Individual job crafting encourages us to adapt our jobs and how we think about them. The beauty of job crafting is that most of the time it doesn't require permission from your boss (although openly discussing job craft-ing is beneficial and, as a boss, encouraging job crafting in your team will help to activate their seeking systems). Whatever our role, we all have some degree of autonomy over the way we do our jobs, and job crafting strategies typically fit into the following categories:

- **When** we do things: adapting our schedules so we can have our best impact. This may be by scheduling tasks that give you energy at the beginning of every day, or scheduling "focus time" (remember Chapter 3) at a time when you are able to do your best work.

- **What** activities we do: reducing, eliminating, increasing, or creating brand new tasks to ensure we are using our strengths and activating our motivations better.
- **How** we do these activities: redesigning tasks to use our strengths and motivations more often in service of the organisational purpose. For example, one client realised he was at his best when co-creating, so he changed the way he gave presentations to better involve the audience.
- **Who** we work with: spending time with those that activate our strengths, or enrich our motivations, and reframing relationships to better deliver on the organisational purpose.
- **Where** we work: choosing our location depending on the type of work we are doing. Distraction-free locations for individual deep work; collaborative spaces for team work; stimulus-rich spaces for creative work.
- **Why** we work: reframing *how we think* about our jobs and specific activities by tapping into our purpose and strengths. Sometimes called "Cognitive Crafting," these are a set of powerful strategies over which we all have complete autonomy – they all happen inside our heads.

How Long Does It Take?

Individual job crafting is a continual process, but the core concepts can be introduced in a three-hour workshop.

Group Size?

Like the rest of the purpose activation journey, this exercise is best done with an intact team of up to 25 people.

How Does It Work?

During the workshop, participants follow a five-step process.

Step One

Participants are introduced to job crafting concepts though examples, like David Holmes, the Southwest airlines flight attendant who raps his safety announcements (look for the video on-line), or Markus Buckingham, the author and CEO who reframed "networking" (which he found energy depleting) as "interviewing" (which used one of his strengths). With a deeper understanding of the concepts, most participants find they have already done some job crafting during their careers and are eager to see what they can do next.

Step Two

David Kelly, the founder of IDEO, famously reviews his calendar on a weekly basis and gives each of his activities a "fun rating" from 1 (please, no) to 5 (I'm *so* fired up by this). He makes a point of removing from his diary anything less than a 4. While most of us don't have that luxury, a review of the main parts of our jobs can uncover useful insights about how we currently spend our time and help identify opportunities for making changes. Therefore, in this step, participants are asked to complete the "Energy Map" table, as shown in Table 7.1.

Activities that participants find they spend large amounts of time on but that don't impact the organisational purpose, don't motivate them, and don't utilise their strengths, are ripe for change. Other opportunities can be found by uncovering activities that do motivate them or utilise their strengths but that they don't typically spend much time on.

Step Three

Have participants think about how to realise the opportunities they have identified by leaning into their strengths. Working in pairs or small groups, have them consider the following strategies, or create their own, to identify what job crafting they will try.

Table 7.1 Energy Map

Label my job components/ activities	Time spent on Activity (H, M, L)	Impact of Activity on Company Purpose (H, M, L)	How much motivation does it give me? (H, M, L)	Current utilisation of Strengths (H, M, L)

When *we do things:*

Strategy	Approach
Focus time	Schedule uninterrupted time to work on your most important work.
Batching	Schedule your most attention-rich tasks when you have a fresh and alert mind (e.g. make all necessary calls in one batch early in the day).
Peaks before troughs	Schedule things you love at the start of a day, or immediately before a task you find more challenging.
Other strategies	Ask yourself these questions to identify additional strategies: • Can I arrange my schedule so I do something I love every day? • Can I schedule more of the tasks that motivate me and use my strengths? • If I do schedule such tasks, should I stop doing others?

What *activities we do:*

Strategy	Approach
Add to your schedule	A bit counter-intuitive, but adding activities you love to your schedule can make you busier but also raise your energy so you get more done.
Follow the warm	"Score" your diary and cut out low-impact/low-energy activity.
Situation selection	Do more of the activities that play to your strengths and motivations.
Other strategies	Create additional strategies by asking yourself, "Can I achieve the desired organisational outcome in a different way, utilising my strengths and motivations?"

How *we do these activities:*

Strategy	Approach
Strength bingo	Plan to complete an important task using as many of your strengths as possible (e.g. intentionally think about how you will apply three or more of your strengths to a key project).

Strategy	Approach
Strength application	Use one of your high-impact strengths in a new way for a week (e.g. using your strength of "empathy" on a new person, or using the strength to help improve the relationship of colleagues, or using the strength in a situation where you historically have not).
Spot false dichotomies	There is always a third way! Find it.
Other strategies	Create additional strategies by asking yourself, "Can I re-think how I do important tasks in a way that uses more of my strengths?"

Who *we do things with:*

Strategy	Approach
Seek and avoid	Seek out radiators (people who radiate and give you energy) and avoid drains (people who sap your energy like a Harry Potter Dementor).
Re-negotiate	Discuss strengths and stress triggers with someone who drains your energy (two-way) and agree on ways of working.
Attention deployment	In a team setting, focus attention on a third person in order to change the dynamic.
Strength enabler	Enable others to us their strengths to change the dynamic.
Other strategies	Ask yourself these questions to identify additional strategies: • Can I change up who I work with on important tasks so I can spend more time with people who energise me? • Can I change the nature of the interactions I have with people who drain my energy?

Where *we do things:*

Strategy	Approach
Location selection	Choose the location based on what brings out your best self during different activities. E.g.: *Walking meetings* – holding 1:1 meetings whilst walking in a different environment. *Quiet Zones* – finding a distraction free location for deep work.

(Continued)

(Continued)

Strategy	Approach
Create theatre	"Dress" the environment (or yourself) to bring the best out of you/your team.
Other strategies	Identify additional strategies by asking yourself what it is about the physical environment that brings the best out of you and make changes accordingly.

Why *we do things (or how to think about what we need to do):*

Strategy	Approach
Labelling	Think about the label you give tasks: Can you change that label to better reflect one of your strengths or motivations? (For example, Markus Buckingham reframing "networking" as "interviewing.")
Laddering	Ask what is the benefit of a task that doesn't motivate me? What is the benefit of *that?* Continue until the benefits have been laddered to something you care about.
Gamification	Turning a low-motivation activity into a game of strengths (e.g. How many times can I display curiosity in this budgeting meeting?)
Dialectic prevention	Spot tasks that cause you concern in advance. Find someone who has a different perspective on the task and schedule 20 minutes to hear and discuss their views.
Context shifting	If your strength is, say, talking 1:1, try to imagine you are talking 1:1 when giving a group presentation, shifting the context.
Invoking identity	Turn your strength into an identity: "I am good at building relationships" becomes "I am a relationship builder." By invoking our identity we are more likely to ignite our seeking systems.

Step Four

In this final step, participants select just one of their opportunities and ideas for changing parts of their job. Have them practice the idea, using their strengths, for three months (see Chapter 9 on purposeful practice to understand how). Encourage participants to continue experimenting with the opportunities they have identified.

Exercise: Team Job Crafting

What Is It?

Team job crafting ignites the seeking system and increases both individual and team effectiveness by allowing employees to choose the work that fulfils them while also satisfying the obligations of the whole team. This is a dilemma faced by many leaders: If I allow every employee to focus just on the things that they find meaningful, will it come at the expense of vital work? This exercise tackles the dilemma head-on and aligns individual and team engagement with organisational success.

How Long Does It Take?

Team job crafting, like individual job crafting, is an ongoing process requiring experimentation and continual improvement. The initial conversation is best undertaken as a half-day "off-site" workshop.

Group Size?

An intact team of up to 25 people

How Does It Work?

Step One

Step one aims to create and clarify team purpose by identifying (or confirming) your team's unique strategic contribution to the organisation's success. The team should seek to answer three questions during this step:

- What do we stand for as a team?
- How will we know we have gotten there?
- How does this contribute to the wider organisational purpose?

Mix and match methods from this book to help the team answer these questions. World Café (Chapter 6), Appreciative Inquiry (Chapter 6), or the "really" re-frame (earlier in this chapter) can each be used. The intention is to provide insight into how the whole team's work combines into their shared contribution while fitting into the broader purpose of the organisation.

Step Two

Identify two or three priorities that can only be completed with input from the *whole team*. These may be priorities for the year or quarter, depending on when the exercise is conducted. Open up participants' minds by asking what you want to collectively accomplish in the time period, and then list all the teams' main tasks required to deliver on those goals. Prioritise the list with the following questions: "Which of our team tasks will have the biggest impact on the organisation?" and "Which of our team tasks require our collective input?" Then, for each priority task, break it down further by identifying the main steps required to deliver it.

Step Three

The individual "Best Self" narratives that each team member created in step 1 of the overall purpose activation journey should now be shared with the group. Participants read both their strengths and their motivations narratives and then post them on the wall for others to refer to throughout the remainder of the exercise. As each person shares their strengths and motivations, have the other participants ask questions to better understand, and learn how to support, them. This part of the exercise amplifies a sense of connection and belonging as everyone feels a personal stake in one another's aspirations.

Step Four

Next, on a flip chart, take the main steps required to achieve the team's priorities (identified in step 2). Now ask each participant to map their motivations and strengths to each of the activities, then explain the reasons why to the rest of the group. It can also be useful to conduct a similar mapping in which individuals allocate themselves to activities based on their role profile or job capabilities.

Step Five

Review the mapping and identify points of interest. Are there activities that need to be done that don't align to anyone's strengths? Are people currently aligned to a task due to their job profile but it does not utilise their strengths? Do several people want to contribute to the same task?

Discussions about these topics are always rich. It's important to remember that all teams will have tasks that someone has to do, though no one really wants to. The power in this step is that you identify the gaps and overlaps in the teams priorities, and how they currently align with the team's strengths and motivations. You are now ready to craft jobs that meet both individual and team needs.

Step Six

Matching individual strengths and passions with strategic commitments is an iterative process. Start with overlaps – those activities where more than one person has a passion – and discuss whether there is value in more than one person being involved. If not, compromises or trade-offs need to be made, such as role rotations or shadowing.

Now explore gaps – those tasks no one really wants. The team can collectively discuss creative ways of making those tasks more desirable using the job crafting strategies discussed earlier in this chapter. Typically teams find ways to take responsibility for that work and are usually far more willing to take it on after having identified other activities that both use their strengths and are strategically important.

Step Three: Highlight the Impact of People's Work

Purpose doesn't only come from big picture issues, like curing diseases or solving world hunger. The feeling of purpose ignites whenever employees and team members can see the cause and effect between their inputs and their team's progress. A sense of purpose soars when they are given the opportunity to use their unique strengths to make a positive impact on others. Likewise, we all feel a sense of purpose when we can experience firsthand how our actions and perspectives become necessary to improving other people's lives and helping them succeed. When leaders highlight their team members' impact, they systematically help employees see and feel how their work affects their customers and the world at large. To get there, the customer must be brought into the heart of the organisation, not just in a metaphorical sense, but in a literal one.

Experiences

As shown in Chapter 5, actual experiences are the key to unlocking insights, connecting emotionally, and igniting the seeking system. So rather than simply pouring over customer feedback scores in order to highlight the impact of your team members' work, bring customers into the organisation and talk to them directly. In a now famous study by Wharton psychologist Adam Grant, fundraisers for college scholarships in a call centre were given the opportunity to meet a scholarship student in person. The student thanked them for their efforts – without which his scholarship would not have been possible – and the fundraisers got to ask him questions. This simple intervention led to the callers spending 142 percent more time on the phone and raising 171 percent more money over a four-week period. There were no such increases for the control groups.[10] There are so many creative ways of bringing customers into the organisation; the trick for leaders is to make this a regular, systematic part of how you do business, not just a one-off event.

Allied Irish Bank (AIB) has a strong purpose to "back [its] customers to achieve their dreams and ambitions." Part of the bank is focused on supporting small businesses, supplying them with access to capital and business banking services. One mechanism AIB uses to provide employees with visibility of the impact of their work is to present them with gifts produced by these small business customers. The gifts also typically come with a personal story from the business about how the bank has been helping it achieve its ambition.

AIB illustrates how organisations need to systematically and creatively find ways to get employees to interact with their customers on a more human level. Whether that's by spending a day in call center operations to better understand the issues customers face, bringing customers into team meetings, sharing inspiring customer stories, or engineering company trips to see how products or services directly impact customers, making that human connection a key strategic imperative emphasises the larger purpose behind an organisation's actions.

Exercise: Your Customer's Customer

What Is It?

This exercise aims to help your team figure out if there are any new tasks they can take on that are both interesting to them and useful to their customers, connecting them more to the impact of their work. Perform this exercise by yourself first to build your awareness of how it works. Then, meet with each of your team members to run the exercise, helping them see the impact of their work.

How Long Does It Take?

Two weeks

Group Size?

One on one, with each of your direct reports.

How Does It Work?

Step One

Have each team member speak with you about the customers they serve. Ask them, "Who are the people who need *your* work to accomplish *their* goals?" Have them think about people they help every day, not just the traditional end customer of the business. For example, a customer might be another employee in the organisation who uses the participant's work to make decisions and improve products.

Step Two

Ask each team member what it is about their work that makes these customers' lives better or worse. Have them write down a side-by-side list covering both. One column should feature the benefits they provide to the customers, and one column should focus on what they do that is potentially making their clients' lives more difficult. Then, underneath the list, have them write down their thoughts on who their customers serve and how their work impacts their customers' customer. This links what they are doing to a broader level of impact.

Step Three

Next, have the participants talk with their customers and directly ask them how the service or product they provide makes their lives better or worse and how it affects *their* customers. Tell them to stay curious and open during these conversations, considering ways to improve whatever the customer experience. Participants should be prepared to report back in two weeks with what they've learned. (By agreeing on a date, you ensure they know this exercise is not an empty one.)

Step Four

When participants return in two weeks, run down what they've learned about their customers, how they're most helpful to them, and what they can do to provide value not just to their direct customers, but to their customers' customers. By recognising the end user (the customers their customers serve), they can better see their impact on a larger scale. Not only will they be able to recognise how to help make their direct customers' lives better, but also how to improve others' experiences down the line.

Summary

- Purpose is personal and emotional. To help employees feel more purposeful, and ignite their seeking systems in turn, they need to be guided through an activation journey consisting of three steps: allow deep reflection, encourage job crafting, and highlight the impact of people's work.
- When allowing deep reflection, team members need to understand their best self and explore their personal purpose before gaining a deeper understanding of their organisational purpose. The Highlights Reel, Identity-Motivations, and the "*really*" reframe exercises can be of help in providing these insights.
- Job crafting is the ability to proactively shape your own work environment such that it fits both your individual needs and those of your team and organisation. Together, individual and team job crafting provide an opportunity for teams, and full organisations, to work to their strengths, values, and aspirations.
- Whenever you help employees and team members see the cause and effect between their inputs, their team's progress, and the impact on customers and beyond, you ignite their feeling of purpose. By focusing on the customers, and hearing directly from them, you further highlight your employees' impact.

Notes

1 Wang, C. (2023) "Women-Led VC Firm Backed By Fashion Billionaire Michael Ying Is Hungry For New Food Tech." *Forbes.*

2 www.heidrick.com/-/media/heidrickcom/publications-and-reports/activating-organizational-purpose.pdf

3 Dutcher, Janine M., J. David Creswell, Laura E. Pacilio, Peter R. Harris, William M.P. Klein, John M. Levine, Julienne E. Bower, Keely A. Muscatell, and Naomi I. Eisenberger (2016) "Self-affirmation activates the ventral striatum: a possible reward-related mechanism for self-affirmation." *Psychological Science* 27, no. 4: 455–466.

4 Rose, Todd, and Ogi Ogas (2018) *Dark Horse: Achieving Success through the Pursuit of Fulfillment.* New York: Harper Collins.

5 Cable, D., and F. Vermeulen (2018, October) "Making work meaningful: a leader's guide." *McKinsey Quarterly.* www.mckinsey.com/business-functions/organization/our-insights/making-work-meaningful-a-leaders-guide

6 Wrzesniewski, Amy, J.M. Berg, A.M. Grant, J. Kurkoski, and B. Welle (2012) "Job crafting in motion: achieving sustainable gains in happiness and performance." In *Annual Meeting of the Academy of Management*, Boston, MA.

7 Leana, Carrie, Eileen Appelbaum, and Iryna Shevchuk (2009) "Work process and quality of care in early childhood education: the role of job crafting." *Academy of Management Journal* 52, no. 6: 1169–1192.

8 Hayes M. (2020) *Global Workplace Study 2020 Full Research Report.* R0130_0920_v3_GWS_ResearchReport.pdf (adpri.org)

9 Shanafelt, Tait D., Colin P. West, Jeff A. Sloan, Paul J. Novotny, Greg A. Poland, Ron Menaker, Teresa A. Rummans, and Lotte N. Dyrbye (2009) "Career fit and burnout among academic faculty." *Archives of Internal Medicine* 169, no. 10: 990–995.

10 Grant, Adam M. (2008) "The significance of task significance: job performance effects, relational mechanisms, and boundary conditions." *Journal of Applied Psychology* 93, no. 1: 108.

PART 4   **Fuel**

Fuel

Introducing Rituals

8

If you've ever been to a wedding reception in the US, a baseball game, or a Fourth of July barbecue after the host has had a few extra drinks, you've probably been roped into a singalong of Journey's *Don't Stop Believing*. Maybe you've even been the one to instigate it. The first chords of the piano intro give way to singer Steve Perry's signature vocals, and by the time the guitar riff flutters in, about a minute later, and the rest of the band follows the lead, you'd be hard-pressed to find a listener who isn't at least humming along, if not fully belting the tune out into the night. Sure, some may argue it's an objectively cheesy song – it came out in 1981, after all – but nothing seems to get certain crowds going quite like this four-minute epic.

In an experiment by Harvard Professor Alison Wood Brooks[1] and colleagues, the researchers asked people to sing this particular song in front of a complete stranger. And though the song is known and loved (though maybe not by *all*), when faced with singing it out loud in such a setting – and not, say, right before closing time at a packed bar – many of us are likely to break out in a cold sweat. To understand the impact that rituals could have on anxiety and performance, participants were asked to undergo a ritual just prior to singing the song, one that was imbued with "magical powers." It went like this:

- Step One: Using a pencil and a piece of paper, draw what you are feeling.
- Step Two: Sprinkle salt on the drawing.
- Step Three: Count to five *out loud*.
- Step Four: Crumple up your paper.
- Step Five: Throw the paper in the trash can.

DOI: 10.4324/9781003396833-13

Singing accuracy improved by more than 12 percent for those who practiced the ritual. Plus, people who performed the ritual reported significantly less anxiety compared to non-rituals. The findings were repeated in a study involving a math test. In this case, the researchers also included a condition where participants were asked to undertake the same pre-performance behaviours, but they were labelled as "random behaviours" rather than a "ritual." Magical powers suddenly lost, this group showed no improvements in either performance or anxiety.

So, Wood Brooks and her colleagues were able to help fuel the seeking system through introduction of a ritual. What gives? What even is a ritual? Does it demand salt and counting? And why can it have such a significant impact on performance? The ritual in these studies was, one could argue, just made-up nonsense. To say it was meaningless, however, would be wrong – *all rituals* are made up. What makes them special is the impact they have on our psychology.

As mentioned in Chapter 4, rituals can be used to help us build our operational frame, but they go even deeper than that. Rituals impart many benefits, reducing our anxiety, building a better sense of community and belonging, improving performance and productivity, making us more creative, and of course, keeping our seeking systems fully fuelled. They also provide a safe space to experiment and help to boost confidence and focus prior to taking on a challenge. Loaded with symbolism and meaning, at their heart, rituals help to make core beliefs concrete and easier to grasp.[2] As such, they are a central backbone to how belief systems operate and a powerful carrier of culture in organisations. As a leader, if you can identify, elevate, and intentionally design successful rituals, introducing them into everyday operations, they will activate your employees' brains' dopamine pathways and help keep seeking systems fuelled across your whole organisation.

What Makes a Ritual?

In the first Wood Brooks study mentioned, she and her colleagues described a ritual as "a predefined sequence of symbolic actions often characterised by formality and repetition that lacks direct instrumental purpose." That's a bit of a mouthful, but it points to some important characteristics that give rituals their power:

- **Predefined sequence:** A ritual should follow a pattern or script, ideally including physical movement and props, as well as language. Reading every night before bed is simply a habit. To elevate that habit to a ritual, you might add a sequence of actions around the act of reading. Maybe before sitting down and picking up a book, you first ensure that, one, your phone is out of the room, so it won't distract you; two, you switch the light on next to your favourite armchair; three, you take a coaster and place it on the coffee table next to the chair, before turning it clockwise four times; and four, using your favourite mug, place a warm drink on the coaster.
- **Symbolic:** For actions to be symbolic, they must first be *intentional*. Being explicit about this intention imbues the actions with meaning. So, if you decide to incorporate a reading ritual before bed, you need to think of it as an actual ritual, in this case maybe a *relaxation* ritual. Paying attention to the steps before settling down to read brings you into the present and primes you for the enjoyment you're about to feel from cosying up with a great book.
- **Formality:** By giving the pattern a degree of formality, it feels more significant than the hundreds of behavioural scripts you unconsciously follow every day. This adds to the symbolism and intentionality described above, helping you to recognise the ritual as a special moment.
- **Repetition:** You may run through the same actions on your daily commute to work (get up, shower, dress, eat breakfast, walk to the station, catch the 7:40 am train to London Victoria, etc.), but this is not a ritual – you're simply following an ingrained pattern of behaviour. When that repetition is combined with the other characteristics, however, you will start to associate it with the intentional benefits of the ritual. Elevating your evening read to the status of a relaxation ritual, for example, will cause you to associate the formal, symbolic, predefined steps with a feeling of relaxation. This connection allows rituals to link the physical with the emotional, bringing these two ways of processing into sync.
- **Lacking instrumental purpose:** This characteristic may seem counterintuitive, but it's important. Completing a sequence or pattern that doesn't make any logical sense appears to switch the brain into a ritualistic thinking mode, causing us to assign meaning to the actions we're performing. Turning a coaster on a coffee table clockwise four

times does not, in itself, improve your evening read, but makes the sequence feel ritualistic.

Rituals are found in every walk of life. They can be individual or collective, frequent or infrequent, religious or secular. Many elite performers in sports adopt pre- and post-performance rituals. Serena Williams bounces the tennis ball exactly five times before her first serve, and exactly two times before her second. The New Zealand Rugby Union team performs an elaborate traditional Māori dance – the Haka – before the start of every match to bring the team together in a moment of unity and prepare them for the game ahead. In a medical setting, many surgical teams pause right after completing the pre-surgery checklist for a silent moment of "reverence" where the nurse reminds the team of who the patient is – someone's spouse, child, parent – and to be considerate of their needs.

Research shows that even simple rituals involving synchronous activity produce positive emotions and weaken the psychological boundaries between the self and a group.[3] As a shared pattern of movement and language, repeated in the same way in a particular situation, rituals can bring groups, teams, and organisation together. In a work setting, there is strong evidence that rituals provide a number of benefits, including how to foster an environment of safety and regulate emotional responses, promote team cohesion, increase feelings of control, and continue fuelling our seeking systems.

Consider the famed animation studio Pixar. The studio has an illustrious history and its many cutting-edge innovations include the production of the world's first computer-animated feature film, *Toy Story*, in 1995. Ed Catmull, the original Pixar co-founder, retired from his role as president of Pixar Animation Studios in 2019, but during his tenure the studio became known for the high levels of support that Pixar employees provided for each other. Nothing exemplified this more than two rituals that characterise how the studio works: the brain trust and the daily review.

The brain trust is a group meeting convened when a director or producer feels they need help on a project, or as Ed Catmull would say, when the movie needs help going from "suck to not suck." They invite other directors and producers, and anyone else they think could be of help, and go over their work in progress. The ritual starts with a screening. Then everyone who has watched the current version withdraws to a conference room for lunch before sitting down to talk. The director and producer stand up and give a summary of where they think they are with the movie, and then they invite feedback.

Candor is a known requirement for a brain trust meeting – everyone is expected to say whatever is on their minds – and no hierarchy exists. After a lively two-hour discussion designed to improve the movie, it is entirely up to the director or producer whether they adopt any of the suggestions made. This ritual has been in place since the making of *Toy Story 2* and continues to this day. It is considered a safe, supportive space and essential to get the best thoughts of the whole studio into the movie.

The daily reviews, or "dailies," serve a similar purpose – they are a ritual for receiving and giving constant feedback in a positive way. Directors and producers show their incomplete work to the whole animation crew, and everyone is invited to comment. Because this is a daily ritual, people get used to sharing unfinished work, overcoming the desire to ensure their work is "good" or perfected before they get outside input. Because dailies are with the entire animation crew, they also serve as a mechanism to disseminate creative ideas that can be built upon by others. Such a ritual, along with the brain trust, can help people to feel a greater sense of control, further reducing fear system activation.

Rituals to Elevate the Seeking System Triggers

While rituals can bring benefits in almost any work setting, in fuelling the seeking system, the focus is on embedding rituals that elevate the core seeking system triggers. That means designing rituals to help your people to personalise purpose, experiment, and self-express.

Rituals to Personalise Purpose

Purpose Reverence

In order for our attitudes to be a good predictor of our behaviours, those attitudes need to be both available and relevant. The purpose reverence ritual allows for a break in the normal routine, pausing to recognise the importance of what is about to happen, appreciating the people involved, and making the company purpose both salient and relevant to the activity.

This short ritual should occur right before a specific event, such as a meeting, a presentation, the start of a work shift, or an important client phone call. The goal is to take a moment to ensure that everyone on the team remembers their personalised purpose prior to starting the activity.

Before the event, the team leader announces the moment of reverence. Everyone stays silent during the moment. The team leader reminds everyone involved of the company, or team, purpose, and their personal commitment to its achievement. Team members are then asked to silently reflect, thinking about how they will bring their best selves to the work at hand in service of the purpose.

Purpose Stories

While working at Heidrick & Struggles, a global leadership advisory firm, I introduced a ritual designed to build a deeper connection to our organisational purpose. The consulting division were passionate about "enabling a world better led." One of our early rituals after launching this purpose was to start our weekly huddle meetings with a five-minute summary of an inspirational leader (living or dead, world statesman to front-line employee, real or fictional). Every team member was charged with identifying and researching a leader on a rotating basis and then presenting their research to the group in the form of a spoken story. Enthusiastic applause and cheering followed every story, at which point the storyteller would choose the team member to relay a narrative the following week.

The ritual was designed to pique interest by introducing something novel every week and helped take the purpose from a "nice statement" to something more meaningful. The ritual also created a safe space where people could self-express about leaders who are important to them and, by extension, their own views about a world better led. Each person had the freedom to tell their stories about whomever and in whatever way they chose. The meeting chair rotated every two-to-three months, creating an opportunity to update the ritual if it was no longer sticking.

Rituals to Experiment

Variables Check

For simple experimentation to become a way of life, try elevating the activity by ritualizing even the most basic of experiments - those that take less than a few hours.

Lets say you want to experiment with a new venue for team drinks. Prior to the event, ask the team to do a light-hearted "variables check":

Q: What is the one thing we want to change about these team drinks?
A: The venue.
This is our independent variable (try to have only one independent variable per experiment).

Q: What change are we expecting to see?
A: Less crowded space, more opportunity to talk as a group, greater connection.
These are our dependent variables.

Q: What stays the same?
A: The people, the timing of the drinks.
These are our controlled variables.

Agree how you are going to measure your variables and then, after the experiment, review the data as a team, using the language of experimentation. Conclude by asking: "what did we learn"? and "what is the next experiment we want to try"?

Flash Walks

When a team constantly brainstorms together in the same room, with the same group of people, these sessions may end up feeling repetitive and uninspiring. To break from this stale repetition, flash walks – accredited to the creative agency BBH – are spontaneous moments designed to smash the tedium. In this ritual, team members working in an office environment take a 20-minute break and go for a walk outside together. Any team member can call a flash walk at any time, with 60 minutes notice.

Attendance is not compulsory, but those working on creative problems benefit from the change in scenery, the physical exercise, and the chance to interact with people that they aren't working with at the moment. The aim is to help people think differently and devise new ideas. All rituals that encourage experimentation should be designed to introduce novelty or "pattern disrupts" (as described in Chapter 5), that help us break out of existing thought processes. When the frontal cortex detects novelty, dopamine levels rise, further fuelling our seeking systems.

Rituals to Encourage Self Expression

Skills Share

The skills share ritual is a quarterly event where team members share projects and skills they have developed, so they can learn from one another and come up with new ideas. By encouraging broad learning across the business, employees can find hidden connections among each other. Critically, the skill share event includes – in fact, encourages – participants to share and appreciate talents they don't usually get to employ at work. For example, people can teach the rest of their team how to dance, cook, draw, or crochet, in addition to work related skills.

The event uses the basic concepts of engaging the seeking system: create a basic infrastructure for the event (the frame), and then allow employees to drive the schedule and content (freedom) through experimentation, self-expression, and personalised purpose. When the skill share event is announced, all employees are invited to become "teachers" and share their new or secret skills with others.

As the leader, you should create a blank "schedule" with windows of 20–30 minutes and enough breakout rooms (physical or virtual) to accommodate the whole team (see the tips from the field box). Next, share the

Tips from the Field

- Try to include enough skills share windows to cover all attendees, such that everybody involved gets the opportunity to share their skill. For instance, for a team of 40, five breakout groups running eight times each in 30-minute windows would be ideal.

- Allow people to sign up for individual skill share windows in advance so popular sessions can be scheduled more than once during the day if need be.

- Appreciate the people sharing their skills by calling out their contributions.

- Mix the day's events with coffee and food breaks, along with other social mixers.

blank schedule with employees and ask those that want to teach a skill to sign up for a window. Not all participants have to be a teacher, but all teachers are participants. Participants choose which sessions they would like to attend. A skills share event typically runs over a half or full day. Team size can vary from 10 to 1,000. The key is that attendees set the schedule and lead the events, with time built in for spontaneity and flexibility.

Recognition Ritual

Finding creative ways to recognise employees can be a powerful way of building psychological safety and encouraging more self-expression. Take BrewDog. Founded in Scotland in 2007, they have become one of the most famous craft beer brewers in the world, operating 50 bars across the UK and 24 internationally. The company was launched in a small industrial warehouse in Edinburgh, where the founders, Martin Dickie and James Watt, accompanied by their pet dog (a chocolate Labrador called Bracken), worked tirelessly to get it off the ground. Dickie famously described the business as "myself and James and a dog," which became the inspiration for the company's name "BrewDog."

As the company has grown, they have created many rituals that continue to remind employees of the entrepreneurial spirit of those founding days, and the special relationship they have with their dog that inspired the company name. For example, BrewDog offers all employees "Pawternity leave," in which everyone is offered a week off when they get a new puppy, with pictures sent around the office to welcome the new arrival.

Organisations' HR functions are often responsible for creative recognition rituals. The online fashion retailer Missguided, for example, realised they didn't always pause to celebrate an employee's job well done, so they introduced their heavily ritualised "Flock Star" award. Nominations go into the "What the Flock" box, and senior management within the team then decide on the winner, who receives a flamingo-shaped trophy and the chance to spin the Happiness Wheel. The wheel is a symbolic prop given special powers. When taken to the employee's desk, spinning it becomes a meaningful event. Wherever the wheel lands denotes a small prize like "hit the snooze button" (a half day's holiday), "a cheeky day off" (a full day's holiday), or even a promise for the boss to make you tea for a week. The team's new recognition strategy, along with other engagement initiatives, contributed to a 30 percent reduction in employee turnover at Missguided over 12 months.[4]

Designing Your Own Rituals

While this chapter shares some examples of rituals that can continue fuelling the seeking system, it's important to adapt, customise, and design new rituals that fit with your organisational context and goals. There are broadly three phases to design and introduce rituals that fuel the seeking system: discovery, elevation, and deployment/scaling. The discovery phase begins by looking for existing habits and routines that already exist and may fit your intention of fuelling the seeking system. If none exist (though they almost always do), then discovery becomes an opportunity to explore new ritual options. In the elevation phase, you look to design the experience in a way that makes the moment meaningful and memorable. Then experimentation comes in during the deployment/scaling phase, when each team refines the experience into one that fits with their context and goals.

Throughout the process, rituals are designed from the bottom up, rather than dictated top down. Rituals cannot just be adopted by decree, and this is especially important when scaling them to other teams and groups within an organisation. A meaningful ritual in one office may feel toe-curlingly embarrassing for a team in another. So, as with every other aspect of scaling seeking system engagement, there is no one-size-fits-all approach to rituals. People must be given freedom to create their own.

Phase One: Discovery

Most individuals, teams, and organisations already have a host of practices and habits that could easily be elevated to ritual status. Brainstorming meetings, "lunch and learn" sessions, Friday afternoon pizzas, morning huddles, after action reviews, quarterly budgeting meetings, new employee onboarding, even your lunchtime walk to your favourite sandwich shop has the possibility to be turned into something more intentional, symbolic, and meaningful. But before these activities can be turned into rituals, they need to be clearly identified. You can begin identifying rituals with your team by running a ritual discovery session. The following exercise for such a session has been tried and tested, but you should feel free to change it to your context, play with it, and make it your own.

Exercise: Ritual Discovery Session

What Is It?

A group discussion that helps uncover two to three existing habits, activities, or practices that can be given special status as rituals.

How Long Does It Take?

60–90 minutes

Group Size?

Five to 20 participants; more if the exercise is run virtually

How Does It Work?

Step One

Introduce the objective for the session: identifying two or three ritual ideas that will help to activate the main seeking system triggers.

Step Two

Warm the group up by getting them immersed in the concept of rituals. First discuss the concepts behind rituals and share the empirical evidence of their impact on performance. Give plenty of examples of rituals to show how they can be fun and inspiring, while producing intangible benefits of enhancing shared purpose, meaning, and community bonds. (You can highlight some of the research and examples referenced in this chapter.) Sometimes people feel uncomfortable with the word "ritual," as they may associate it with religious institutionalism, or even some form of corporate brainwashing. If that's the case with your team, try using alternative phrasing like "tradition," "custom," or "celebration."

Step Three

Get the team to recognise *individual* rituals that may already exist in their lives. This helps them to realise that all of us partake in rituals – or at least in moments that have the potential to be elevated to ritual status – and encourages them to start "thinking in rituals." Start by asking everyone to consider their typical workday, from the time they wake up to the time they go to bed. As they think through their day, tell them to capture any individual rituals on stickies.

These could include stopping at their favourite coffee shop on the way to work, or doing a two-minute yoga routine at their desks in between each meeting. Everyone's rituals will be different. Some may occur less frequently than others, so also ask the team to think through rituals that may happen every month, quarter, or year. For example, maybe some team members always take a day off on their birthdays, or they may catch up on missed admin during quiet periods throughout the month or year.

Step Four

Next, using different coloured stickies than those for personal rituals in step three, ask participants to think about *collective* rituals at work and write them down. Have them consider moments of transition (e.g., promotion celebrations, new employee onboarding, or farewell lunches) and any current team traditions, ceremonies, or customs (e.g., annual company ski trip or last Friday of the month bar trivia). Does the team have any mantras, formal or informal? If so, when are they enacted? Think about common working practices or routines too. Ask the team to post all their stickies on a flip chart and discuss them. You may get something like the image shown in Figure 8.1 (white are the individual rituals, grey the collective):

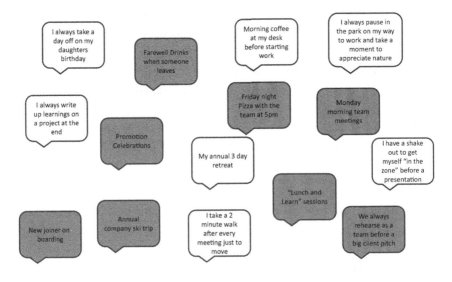

Figure 8.1

Individual and Collective Rituals

The idea is to help the team recognise that rituals, or the potential for rituals, exist in all parts of our work lives.

Step Five

Now ask the team to consider whether any of the rituals identified in the previous step address, or have the potential to address, the main seeking system triggers. Draw a simple table on a flip chart, as shown in Figure 8.2, and ask the team to re-post their stickies in the categories shown. The key question is whether any of these existing rituals currently elevate the seeking system triggers, or whether with some design work, they could do. Not every existing ritual will naturally map, as they may have different intentions, but that's OK.

Step Six

Though this exercise is an excellent way to uncover existing rituals, you may find they just don't cut it – even those that you think can be spruced-up and made more intentional and symbolic. If that's the case, you and your team may want to create brand new ones. To start, add to the list in Figure 8.2 by brainstorming ideas under each of the headings. Consider asking the following prompting questions of participants to get them brainstorming around new rituals based on each trigger:

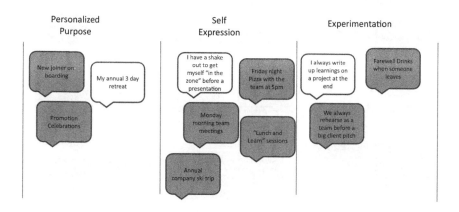

Figure 8.2

Mapping Rituals to Seeking System Triggers

Personalised Purpose

- What opportunities exist that can exhibit the impact of our work on our customers?
- How can we deepen our understanding of our organisational purpose?
- How do we celebrate our best work?

Self-Expression

- How can we build more of a team identity?
- What team rituals would help us all to speak up?
- What opportunities do we have to demonstrate inclusion?

Experimentation

- What opportunities currently exist to experiment?
- Since failure is an important part of experimentation, how do we acknowledge and recognise failure?
- How do we capture what we have learned from our mistakes while experimenting?

Your expanded list may look something like those shown in Figure 8.3 (new ideas shown in black).

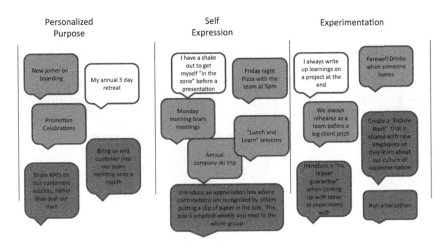

Figure 8.3

Potential Additional Rituals

Step Seven

Now prioritise two or three rituals that could be elevated and given special status. Ask the team to consider key questions for ritual selection. These could vary depending on your culture and context, but will likely include the following:

* Should we prioritise individual or group rituals?
* How often do we want to perform our rituals?
* What is more important to our group right now: Do we want to dial-up personalised purpose, self-expression, or experimentation?

With these basic criteria established, ask each team member to vote on their top three rituals. Discuss the choices as a group and settle on those your team would like to observe moving forward. Before they can be considered full-on rituals, though, they must first be elevated.

Phase Two: Elevation

Elevating routines or habits into rituals, or taking a concept and developing it into one, requires designing the experience in a way that makes the moment meaningful and memorable. The flow of the ritual needs to be identified during the elevation phase, featuring a defined beginning, middle, and end.

Exercise: Ritual Elevation Session

What Is It?

A group discussion to design a moment or activity that can be given special status as a ritual, fuelling one or more of the seeking system triggers.

How Long Does It Take?

60–90 minutes

Group Size?

Five to 20 participants; more if the exercise is run virtually

How Does It Work?

Start by reminding the group of the ritual intention, design criteria, and design considerations from Phase One. Then, in small groups, have participants create a "ritual script," which should define the essential sequence, location, timing, props, language, and actions into the flow of the ritual. As an example, let's say you wanted to introduce a "hackathon" into your organisation as a way of encouraging more experimentation, and then elevate the process into a ritual. Keeping the intention, design criteria, and design considerations in mind, you would complete the template in Table 8.1 as shown.

Keep working the ritual script until the team are happy that it will work for your context and that it fulfils the design criteria. Notice that what is *not needed* here to create a new ritual is a lot of money. Rituals don't need big budgets, which is partially what allows them to scale.

Phase Three: Deploy and Scale

To deploy and scale, start with iteration. Iterating is a way of improving your ritual design by testing whether it works in practice. To iterate, "roleplay" the ritual together with your team. Try experimenting with different design considerations: change the physical space, use different props, try out new language, try new physical movements. Keep repeating this roleplaying until you find a ritual that resonates with the whole group. From there, rituals can begin being scaled into regular practices across a whole enterprise, following the key scaling principles detailed in Chapter 2. As discussed, a frame must first be built to set a context for people to perform the ritual in their own way. This concept follows the idea of a "co-creation vehicle," meaning teams are supported with a framework but given the freedom to decide what the ritual is and how to do it.

A good way to begin scaling is to introduce quarterly ritual design sessions as one of your organisation's key rituals. By connecting these sessions to, say, the quarterly budgeting cycle, you'll find that ongoing ritual review and design becomes part of your culture and how you keep the seeking system fuelled. Getting rituals off the ground and integrated at more than just an individual or team level also requires a willingness for people to suspend analytical thinking and bring out others' creativity and playfulness. Identify teams whose seeking systems are already engaged and seek out these team leaders to pilot the three-phase ritual design process.

Table 8.1 Ritual Elevation Template

Ritual Intention	Design Criteria	Design Considerations
Continual fuel for the seeking system through activation of the following trigger (identify): • Self-Expression • Experimentation • Personalised Purpose	• Follows a predefined sequence • Symbolic • Formal • Repetitive • Lacking instrumental purpose	• Physical space • Props, objects • Language • Context and time • Action or movement

Ritual Script

Sequence	*Timing*	*Props*
1. Everyone on the team is informed of the date, the duration, and the purpose of the hackathon. The clear, necessary problem to be solved is framed on the invitation as a challenge: How can we solve (this problem) in three hours?	One month before the event	E-mail invitation with stand-out banner
2. Set up a chat room for participants to communicate digitally and stay in touch after the event.	Three days before the event	
3. Set up a physical venue.	One day before the event	• Usual workshop props, including flip charts, pens, post-it notes, etc.
4. Facilitator or team leader can help form sub-teams and introduce people who don't normally work together.	30 minutes	
5. Teams work the problem at banquet tables, recording their ideas directly on the tablecloths.	60 minutes	
6. In the final 30 minutes the facilitator rings a bell and all don baseball caps embossed with the company logo.	30 minutes	
7. Sub-teams (if there are any) share what they have done and make a commitment to the next step.	20 minutes	
8. Play music to commemorate that the problem has been solved.	10 minutes	

161

Summary

- Rituals reduce anxiety, build a better sense of community, improve performance, produce creativity, and keep seeking systems fully fuelled. They also provide a safe space to experiment and boost confidence and focus prior to taking on a challenge. They are central to how belief systems operate and a powerful carrier of culture in organisations.
- If you can identify, elevate, and intentionally design successful rituals, they will activate your employees' brains' dopamine pathways, keeping seeking systems fuelled across your whole organisation.
- The following characteristics give rituals their power: they have a predefined sequence, they are symbolic, they are formal, they require repetition, and they lack instrumental purpose.
- Include rituals with your team that fuel all three of the seeking system triggers – rituals to personalise purpose, to experiment, and to encourage self-expression. These may include purpose reverence and purpose stories, flash walks, skill shares, and recognition rituals.
- In addition to incorporating rituals into your teams' processes, you can also develop new ones from the ground up through a three-phase process of discovery, elevation, and deploying and scaling.

Notes

1 Brooks, Alison Wood, Juliana Schroeder, Jane L. Risen, Francesca Gino, Adam D. Galinsky, Michael I. Norton, and Maurice E. Schweitzer. "Don't stop believing: Rituals improve performance by decreasing anxiety." *Organizational Behavior and Human Decision Processes* 137 (2016): 71–85.

2 Durkheim, Emile (1957) *The Elementary Forms of the Religious Life* (trans. J.W. Swain). London: Allen and Unwin.

3 Hobson, Nicholas M., Juliana Schroeder, Jane L. Risen, Dimitris Xygalatas, and Michael Inzlicht. "The psychology of rituals: An integrative review and process-based framework." *Personality and Social Psychology Review* 22, no. 3 (2018): 260–284.

4 Reward Gateway Integrations (2023) *Missguided* Reward Gateway Integrations. www.rewardgateway.com/uk/case-study/employee-recognition-missguided

Practicing the Triggers

"This is unlike anything we've done before," a senior HR director I worked with recently proclaimed. She and her HR leadership team were on a journey to activate their best selves, using a process similar to the one described in Chapter 7. They had deepened their understanding of their unique gifts and strengths and explored creative ways of applying them to their biggest challenges. The experience had been a meaningful one for the HRD and her team. More used to a "deficit" model of development where they were encouraged to focus primarily on improving weaknesses, such an intimate and powerful reveal of their strengths was a new experience. She and her team described the workshop in various ways: unexpected; creative; energetic; magical at times; human; dynamic; full of laughter and tears, as well as uncertainties; challenging; beautiful; life-giving and life-changing; a bit scary; and hard work. Regardless of these varying and sometimes contradictory feelings, one thing the team was certain about was that at the end of the workshop, their seeking systems felt fully engaged.

Like many workshops or training sessions, this one concluded with each participant making personal commitments about what they were going to take from the experience and apply to the workplace. But four weeks later, when asked about how they had fared since then, this is what one of the team members had to say:

That workshop was one of the most impactful interventions I have experienced. I was so motivated to start using my strengths more every day, but then work got in the way. I was faced with the same pressures and routines and just slipped back into my old way of working. I had

DOI: 10.4324/9781003396833-14

been encouraged to practice my strengths, and I have done so a little, but I just haven't had the time to really focus on it yet.

This experience is far from unique. Fitting every activity and best intention into our busy schedules is challenging. And no matter how profound a learning experience is for us, new insights and their associated emotional rush can soon dissipate unless we consistently pay attention to them – and this isn't always easy. This takes us back to the concept of *attention density*, discussed in Chapter 1. The greater the concentration on a specific idea or thought process, the higher the attention density. With enough attention density, our thoughts can become an intrinsic part of our identity, changing the way we see ourselves, perceive the world, and even how our brains work.

But what does it actually take to increase our attention density on our seeking system triggers? There's just no getting around it – it takes practice. Although many of us view practice as dull and repetitive, it can be pure rocket fuel for the seeking system if designed in a way that activates all its triggers. In the context of practice, self-expression means using our unique strengths, experiences, and ideas to make a practice relevant to us so we can internalise new ideas. Experimentation offers a low-risk way to practice a newly acquired skill, "learning by doing," so we can receive quick feedback and adjust accordingly. Personalised purpose means having a clear improvement goal, so our practice is intentionally designed around a purpose we connect to. To continue to fuel the seeking system, then, individuals need to take specific steps to keep getting better at what they do.

Unfortunately, the concept of practice is not embedded in most businesses. Most of us are so busy "performing," trying to add value to our enterprise, we rarely "practice" to get better. If practice is encouraged, it is often reserved for short periods of acquiring new knowledge and learning new skills, without a focus on continuous development. What's needed, instead, is a way of embedding practice into every working day, so as to keep the seeking system fuelled and help create a vibrant organisation.

What Is Practice?

Is there such a thing as poor practice? According to the late, great, Swedish psychologist Anders Ericsson the answer is definitely *yes*. Ericsson dedicated his career to the study of expert performance, finding that expertise in domains such as music, chess, medicine, and sports can be improved through what he termed "deliberate practice." He found that what most people view as practice – lots of repetition of activities they normally do – results in a plateauing of performance. At that point behaviours become automatic, but no further improvement takes place. Deliberate practice, however, is much more intentional and follows a set pattern:

- Set well-defined, specific goals for learning
- Break them down into smaller chunks
- Create a plan for achieving each chunk
- Focus hard on the improvement goal
- Receive immediate feedback on your performance (ideally from an expert coach)

In the context of fuelling the seeking system your practice should be *strengths* based, experimental, and in service of your purpose. That means finding creative ways to purposefully apply your strengths to your challenges and development needs. Committing to being a lifelong learner – always exploring, experimenting, and refining your strengths – can fuel your seeking system for the long term.

Practicing the Triggers in the Workplace

When you think about professional sports, it's easy to see how practice becomes a core part of performance. It's unthinkable that an NBA championship team, for example, would be successful without practicing. Plus, the time spent actually "performing" – playing games against other teams – are relatively short. Depending on the sport, some teams may play one competitive game per week, meaning they may spend 90 percent or more of their time practicing, and just 10 percent or less performing.

In business, this ratio is, at best, reversed and is often much, much worse. Employees are so busy doing their jobs, they often feel they don't have – or are not allowed – the time to practice their skills in a deliberate way. For many, the only time formally designated for "practice" is during training programs. And in the UK, for instance, the average employee receives fewer than seven training days *per year*.[1] For a full-time employee, that equals around 3 percent of their working time.

"Practice" in a business context is rarely given a specific focus either. It is often just assumed that employees will practice what they learn in the course of performing their duties. Learning and development professionals have long advocated for a more holistic approach to learning, stipulating a ratio of 70:20:10 as the ideal. This suggests 70 percent of your learning should be done "on the job," 20 percent through coaching, and 10 percent through formal training programs. But even this model can be limiting. Despite 70:20:10 advocating 70 percent of learning on the job, the lion's share of investment is typically funnelled into the 10 percent or 20 percent that is formal training programs and coaching, respectively. It is too often assumed that the 70 percent of learning on the job will just magically happen, without any intervention required. Instead, a more structured approach to practice is required. That approach starts with the introduction of "practice zones."

Practice Zones

One way you can scale up practice is by providing structures that simply give employees the time and space to do it. This advice may sound like common sense, but it sure is not very common in organisational life. By encouraging practice and providing the appropriate resources, leaders can reduce burnout, improve work contributions, and help their organisation thrive. To turn normal business activities into opportunities to practice your strengths or other seeking system triggers, you need to develop practice zones. Practice zones are designated time and spaces where you and your team give yourselves the opportunity to be intentional about improvement. That intentionality, applied regularly, provides ongoing fuel for the seeking system. A practice zone has three distinct characteristics: the frame, playfulness, and feedback.

The Frame

Before entering the practice zone, be intentional about how you are going to use the time by building a frame, as discussed in Chapter 4. By using a frame to design the practice zone, its boundaries in time and space stay intact. The practice zone has a beginning and an end, and should provide clarity on the desired results, rules, routines, and resources, the four Rs of the frame. Let's say you have decided you want to practice "closing" sales with clients. At first sight you may think there are no opportunities for this type of practice other than by actually interacting with a real customer. By building the frame, however, you are able to start creating an effective practice zone:

- **Results:** There are many different strategies for closing sales. In this case, say you want to improve your use of "question closes" during sales meetings. An example of a question close is, "In your opinion, does what I am offering solve your problem?" You also want to practice using different strategies in different contexts to learn the best time to use which strategy.
- **Resources:** You are going to have a colleague attend all sales meetings with you and ask her to provide specific feedback on your question closes.
- **Routines:** You are going to introduce a pre-meeting to roleplay the sales meeting with your colleague, plus an immediate "after action review" following the customer meeting. The after-action review will include another roleplay to reinforce what you're learning. This type of playful activity will help you further prepare for real-life question closes.
- **Rules:** The pre-meetings and after action reviews will become safe and playful practice zones. You will continue practicing "question closes" for one month.

In this example, the two other distinct characteristics of practice zones come up: playfulness and feedback. These are equally as important as the frame itself.

Playfulness

To enter the practice zone is to enter a different kind of space, a different dimension almost, where the rules of ordinary business life are temporarily suspended. Temporarily "suspending reality" in this way creates a safe place where employees can engage in behaviour that might otherwise feel risky or uncomfortable in the "real world." Practice zones therefore provide the perfect opportunity to incorporate "play" into business activities. The playfulness associated with practice zones has an almost immediate positive impact – even the anticipation of laughing has been shown to decrease cortisol and norepinephrine by 39 percent and 70 percent, respectively, making us feel safer, calmer, and less stressed.[2]

In recent years, organisations have recognised the importance of play in learning and development, and there's nothing quite like it when it comes to fuelling seeking systems. Play has long been observed in the natural world, and evidence supports that playful activity functions to help develop sophisticated cognitive and behavioural abilities.[3] Research has also found evidence that play at work is linked with less fatigue, boredom, stress, and burnout in individual workers.[4] Play is positively associated with job satisfaction, sense of competence, and creativity. And when a task is presented playfully, participants are more involved and spend more time on the task.

And the proof doesn't end there. Research also suggests that the upsides of play extend *beyond the individual*. When teams are playful, they benefit from increased trust, bonding and social interaction, a sense of solidarity, and a decreased sense of hierarchy. And play at work can benefit whole organisations by creating a friendlier work atmosphere, higher employee commitment to work, more flexible organisation-wide decision making, and increased organisational creativity.

Playful practice can be incorporated in a number of ways. *Competitive play* creates a reward system in the practice. For example, if you successfully include three different closing strategies into a single roleplay practice, you can reward yourself with pizza for lunch. Or consider some *exploratory play*, based on learning through research. You could, say, research at least three tried and tested closing questions per week and use them all in the practice zone over five days. There is also an opportunity to build in *creative play*. In this case, maybe experiment with at least one brand new closing strategy that you have created every time you enter the practice zone.

The trouble with play is that many leaders think it is somehow frivolous and doesn't actually contribute to productivity or increased performance. In service of an "attractive" workplace, they may install a ping-pong table, foosball table, or PlayStation. They may even throw some beanbags and LEGOs in the corner of the break room, but they secretly don't really want people to use them. (What they really want is for their employees to get back to work.) That is why making *work* playful is a better way of integrating play into the workplace. And incorporating this playfulness into your practice zones is a great way to do so.

Feedback

No meaningful improvement can be possible without feedback, and the foundation of all feedback is accurate observation and measurement. It is only through measurement that we have any proof of whether we are getting better or worse at the activity we are practicing. Notice how a practice zone exists *within the context of work*. It is not a training course conducted outside your normal place of work. Not only does this provide a more immediate opportunity for practice, but also for feedback on that practice.

Let's say you have an internal meeting coming up with your team. It's already a safe environment, and you may decide to declare the meeting a "practice zone" so you can deliberately practice including team members in the conversation, a strength you want to further develop. You keep that declaration to yourself – only you know the meeting is now a practice zone for you. In this scenario, you reflect on your own progress after the meeting through journaling.

Journaling has been scientifically shown to stimulate our personal growth.[5] The process increases attention density on our experiments and experiences with new behaviours. Moreover, writing accesses and occupies our left brain, the analytical and rational part, freeing up our right brain to create, intuit, and feel. As a result, journaling allows us to track patterns and trends, clarify our thoughts and feelings, and solve problems more effectively.

While individual practice is good, it is difficult to both practice a task and measure your progress at the same time, so having a good coach to track progress, provide feedback, and help you create practice strategies can be effective. That may mean asking a colleague to observe your practice zone and provide feedback immediately after the meeting. You could then swap roles and, at the next meeting, you become the observer and coach while they practice. Or you could declare to the whole team that you want the meeting to act as a practice zone. At the start of the meeting, each participant should state what they want to practice. Then, set aside time at the end of the meeting for participants to provide specific feedback to each other.

Embedded Practice Zones

Robert Schaffer has written about his work with United Aluminum of New Haven, Connecticut. This shows how building practice zones into "business as usual" can benefit organisations. In the 1990s, about 20 percent of United's orders were shipped late, causing severe problems for their customers. United provided components that went into other companies' manufacturing processes, so late delivery meant they were becoming a bottleneck. The company tried to fix the issue by investing in new processing control systems, but the problems still persisted.

In response, United invited all employees to join in on an experiment, one that utilised the concept of practice zones (although they weren't specifically called "practice zones"). They selected a target week about six weeks out and gave the whole company the radical goal of *zero* late shipments for that target week. In the run-up to that target week, everyone at the company – employees, supervisors, engineers, and salespeople – started to apply the principles of deliberate practice. They broke down their own jobs into smaller chunks and looked for any opportunities that would contribute to shipping on time; they focused on those improvement goals; and they continued to practice and experiment using real time feedback to guide their efforts.

The company tested dozens of innovations. When the target week came, 100 percent of the orders went out on time. The same thing happened the following week. Running small practice experiments in what were effectively practice zones started to become habitualised. The seeking systems of the whole organisation were continually fuelled and, since that first target week, delivery reliability at the company has never gone below 95 percent.[6]

In another example, IMI, the precision engineering company based in the UK, has also incorporated the principles of purposeful practice to a core business process – their induction of new employees. At IMI, induction was not viewed as a one-off event, but designed as a virtual journey over a six-month period. The intention was to make induction an immersive experience and frame it around a series of playful challenges designed to engage the seeking system while inducting new hires into the culture of the organisation.

Typically, organisations view induction as an opportunity to fill the new joiner with as much organisational knowledge as possible in the shortest possible time. The idea is to accelerate the time it takes for new employees to become fully productive. Many new joiners describe the induction process as "drinking from a firehose." But as those of us who ever crammed for an exam can testify, this is not the best way of retaining knowledge for the long term.

IMI realised that core company information about products, services, policies, and performance standards were all available online. Accessing this information required getting used to the company's IT systems (and that very much required practice). So, IMI removed all the usual presentations from the induction sessions, and instead gave new joiners a series of "detective tasks" to complete over the course of several weeks. These playful challenges required new joiners to use the IT systems to find key pieces of information about the company, providing them with both practice of the systems and new knowledge.

Practice zones can be institutionalised, as with United Aluminum and IMI, but they can also be introduced by individual workers. Introducing the concepts of practice zones through training programs or via your line manager network can provide the permission, skills, and motivation for individuals to develop their own practices. For example, employees can decide on three or four meetings or activities per week that they want to designate as practice zones. Better still, they can work with their teams to agree what they are practicing and who will be providing feedback.

After a time, the phrase "practice zone" becomes short hand for a clear set of behavioural rules that the team understands. Psychologists call these rules an "existing schema" – after it's established you don't have to carefully explain the ground rules for the interaction; those rules are well understood in a simplified statement. Those rules are also different from the normal rules of working life as they apply only when you and your team members are in a practice zone. For individuals and teams to continue to fuel the seeking system, however – whether they're in a practice zone or not – they must turn practice into a habit.

Make Practice a Habit

Aristotle famously told us that excellence is a habit, not an act. Achieving excellence requires practice and, even with practice zones, finding opportunities to regularly practice in the workplace can sometimes be challenging. Fortunately, there are science-backed strategies that can help us incorporate practice in the workplace until it becomes a full-on habit. The following strategies can help you kick-start your practice, make you more likely to follow through on each practice session, and keep you committed in the long run.

Kick-Start Your Practice

They say that the first step is always the hardest, and that is often true when making a change to established work patterns. Introducing practice zones can be challenging, and sometimes we need to give ourselves (and others) a nudge to get going. Fortunately, there are a range of science-backed techniques that can help.

Harness the Fresh Start Effect

Behavioural scientist Katy Milkman of the Wharton School recommends using "fresh starts" to increase your motivation to change. Choose a date that marks a new beginning, either because it is a particular landmark (start of a new financial year or a work anniversary, for example) or because it is triggered by a significant event, such as a change of company strategy or year-end results. Use that moment to help you and your team commit to a predetermined practice. Whether employees decide what skills they want to practice individually, or if they agree to them after a group brainstorming discussion, once identified, tie the beginning of the practice to a fresh start. Fresh starts have been shown in some studies to boost optimism about the future and increase the likelihood of following through on a goal by 20 to 30 percent.[7]

Schedule Practice

Chapter 3 discussed the importance of normalising focus time as a way of reducing cognitive load. Focus time is the ability to work distraction free on important tasks for a defined period. By scheduling 60-minute practice zones in the same way you schedule focus time, you signal their importance. Scheduling in this way also acts as a pledge that this is important, and as such, increases commitment to the goal.

Build Micro Habits

If scheduling a 60-minute practice session feels like too much at first, try introducing a three-minute practice session instead. This is an example of a micro habit, a tiny action you can build upon to create a full-fledged habit. Begin with a step so small that it easily overcomes any resistance to starting, and failure becomes nearly impossible. Research shows it is more effective to make smaller more frequent commitments than larger infrequent ones. If your goal is to do 100 push-ups per day, for example, you could start with committing to one simple push-up per day. If your goal is to practice writing every day, commit to writing one word. If you want to encourage your team to practice their unique strengths every day, introduce a five-minute purposeful practice session. As starting is often the biggest barrier to a new behaviour, once you get going your five minutes may become 15. As you naturally layer on more each day – whether push-ups, ideas, or time – you will slowly build closer to your goal. Eventually you will develop a routine and the habit will become ingrained.

Follow Through

While the first step may well be the hardest, life still has a habit of tripping us up when it comes to following through on our commitments. Just having practice scheduled does not guarantee you will follow through, but the following techniques can help you remain focused on completing your practice sessions.

Use Action Triggers

Also known as "implementation intentions" or "cue-based planning," action triggers link a new behaviour to a specific event in "when-then" or "if-then" statements. For example: "When I arrive at work Monday, before turning on my computer, then I will take 20 minutes and think about the highest leverage things I can achieve today." Or "If I think a client's requests might be heading down the wrong path, then I will ask 'Do you mind if I ask a question about that direction?'" By linking actions in this way, you create triggers and you pre-load the decision to practice behaving in a certain way. This approach conserves energy because you allow features of the environment to help you appropriately manage your behaviour.

Action triggers are also useful when the strength you want to practice cannot be neatly encapsulated in a practice zone without some form of role-play. You may, for example, want to improve on incorporating empathy to diffuse conflict, but you never know when conflict is going to occur. In such cases, rather than a practice zone, you should use an action trigger: "When I experience conflict in one of my interactions, then I will practice listening carefully and calmly to their point of view before reacting."

Timely Reminders

For an intention to become an actual behaviour, it must be both relevant and available. A timely reminder to prompt your practice – right before you're meant to get started – can help you follow through on your intentions. Research shows that reminders that aren't timely have far smaller benefits.[8] One way to incorporate timely reminders is to send them to yourself. The gym chain Virgin Active experimented with this approach by installing "video booths" in some of its facilities. Members would enter the video booth just after a workout when they were on an "exercise high" with their endorphins still pumping. They would record a video encouraging themselves to visit the gym tomorrow, and they were able to schedule the release of the video such that it arrived on their smartphone at precisely the right time the following day.

In another example, Dan Cable and Michael Parke of London Business School and I ran a study where we attempted to encourage 2,240 employees of the Consulting Firm PwC in the UK to practice speaking up (either challenging poor behaviour when they saw it or voicing improvement opportunities). Each Monday morning, participants were given a timely reminder to access an online portal to learn about and practice a single activity related to increasing employee voice. Then, each Friday, they received another reminder to reflect on their thoughts and feelings from that week's exercise. Because we designed the intervention to be run via an online platform, it didn't rely on coaches or managers to convince employees to keep at it, nor did they need to be involved at all. That meant the intervention could be scaled indefinitely throughout an organisation.

The online platform, which was designed to encourage learning and purposeful practice through timely reminders, enabled successful fuelling of the seeking system. Our results showed that those that had practiced speaking up had 16 percent higher empowerment scores, and 2 percent higher utilisation. Moreover, they felt 12 percent more inspired, were 7 percent less cynical to change, felt 10 percent less anxious, and 15 percent less bored.

Stay Committed

As mentioned, for your practice zones to become part of an established way of working, they must become habitual. This means staying committed for long enough that the behaviour gets adopted without it taking conscious effort. The one-two combination of streaks and exceptions can help you stay committed.

Streaks

When it comes to staying committed to your practice, keep track of the number and quality of your practice sessions. Once you have completed a few practice sessions in a row, you start to develop what is known as a "streak." The more sessions you complete, the longer your streak. This data can motivate you to continue developing your habit.

For instance, the popular social media app Snapchat enables users to post photos and videos that disappear from the site after a few moments. Images captured or viewed within Snapchat are known as "snaps," and the app makes full use of the science of streaks in encouraging users back to the app. A Snapchat streak is when you send direct snaps back and forth with a friend for a number of consecutive days. Every day you send a Snap to a friend, your streak gets longer. Snapchat will reward longer streaks with emojis: the 100 emoji is used to mark streaks lasting 100 days, while a mountain emoji is awarded for an exceptionally long streak (small rewards lead to the release of dopamine, which as you know by now, fuels your seeking system). Once you've started a streak, you feel motivated to continue.

I still vividly remember my four kids standing in the rain outside my neighbour's house so they could "borrow" their WiFi signal. Our own WiFi had dropped and they would rather have gotten wet, cold, and uncomfortable than break their Snapchat streaks! Streaks are an important commitment device, as anything more than a short lapse in your practice can prevent the new habit from forming. Allowing yourself such short lapses, however, is important as well.

Emergency Passes

The "what the hell?" effect can be found in any sort of goal-setting or will-power task – once we give in to some type of behaviour we're trying to avoid, we may say, "well, why bother?" and end up giving up. Numerous experiments have shown that even small failures can lead to a downward spiral of behaviour. Break your streak on Snapchat and you may suddenly find yourself not using the app for a month; eat one cookie when you set yourself a goal not to eat any and you might find yourself eating the whole jar. Now if you want to restrict social media use then breaking your streak could turn out to be a good strategy. In the context of staying committed to practice, however, it can be a disaster.

Thankfully, research by Marissa Sharif and Suzanne Shu[9] has given us a powerful technique to countering the "what the hell" effect: allow yourself some emergency passes. By making explicit allowances for those times when our will power waivers or life just gets in the way, our self-confidence and desire to continue a practice survives. In the Sharif and Shu study, participants who were asked to complete a task every day for seven days, but when given two emergency passes, were more than twice as likely to complete the task than those given the same task and no passes. Using this approximate ratio feels about right for most meaningful tasks. So, for example, if you are aiming for four quality practice zones per week, allow for one emergency pass per week – this gives you some flexibility while still making sure you stay on task and turn the planned habit into a practice.

Summary

- Though often overlooked in a business setting, practice is imperative to continuous improvement and learning, which can majorly fuel the seeking system if designed in a way that activates all its triggers.
- Practice zones provide a safe, convenient space for employees to dedicate time to practice. These zones have three distinct characteristics: the frame, playfulness, and feedback. Examples of successful practice zones prove how they can be institutionalised or developed from the ground up. Using the term "practice zone" can, after time, cue people into adopting the required characteristics. As such, declaring a meeting a "practice zone" immediately changes the rules of that meeting so people can intentionally practice.
- To make practice a habit, kick start the practice by harnessing the fresh start effect and scheduling practice zones. Make new practices easy to start by using micro-habits.
- To continue embedding the habit, follow through with your practice using action triggers and timely reminders.
- Keep going by starting a streak and allowing yourself some emergency passes.

Notes

1 UKCES (2011) *Employer Investment in Training.* UKCES. https://assets.publishing.service.gov.uk/government/uploads/system/uploads/attachment_data/file/306433/ukcess13-employer-investment-in-training.pdf

2 Berk, Lee S., Stanley A. Tan, and Dottie Berk. "Cortisol and Catecholamine stress hormone decrease is associated with the behaviour of perceptual anticipation of mirthful laughter." (2008): 946–11.

3 Kerney, M., J. B. Smaers, P. T. Schoenemann, et al. (2017) "The Coevolution of Play and the Cortico-cerebellar System in Primates." *Primates* 58: 485–491. https://link.springer.com/article/10.1007/s10329-017-0615-x

4 Petelczyc, Claire Aislinn, Alessandra Capezio, Lu Wang, Simon Lloyd D. Restubog, and Karl Aquino (2017) Play at work: an integrative review and agenda for future research. *Journal of Management* 44, no. 1: 161–190.

5 Wilson, T. (2013) *Redirect: Changing the Stories We Live By.* London: Penguin.

6 Schaffer, R. H. (2016) "To Get Better at Your Job, Work Practice into Your Routine." *Harvard Business Reviews*, January 29. https://hbr.org/2016/01/to-get-better-at-your-job-work-practice-into-your-routine.

7 Beshears, John, Katherine Milkman, Hengchen Dai, and Shlomo Benartzi (2021) "Using fresh starts to nudge increased retirtement savings." *Organizational Behavior and Human Decision Processes* 167: 72–87.

8 Austin, John, Sigurdur O. Sigurdsson, and Yonata S. Rubin (2006) "An examination of the effects of delayed versus immediate prompts on safety belt use." *Environment and Behavior* 38, no. 1: 140–149.

9 Sharif, Marissa and Suzanne Shu (2017) "The benefits of emergency reserves: greater preference and persistence for goals that have slack with a cost." *Journal of Marketing Research* 54, no. 3: 495–509. DOI:10.1509/jmr.15.0231.

10 | **Inspiring Performance**

When Tess McGregor became CEO of a closed pension fund managing over £100billion of client savings, she had a number of goals in mind. She wanted to keep the book of savings broadly the same but streamline operations, reduce costs by leveraging digital, and make the environment "the best place to work." Over her career, Tess (real person, fake name) had gained an excellent understanding of technology and had led business areas with a consumer focus. While she didn't have a background in the industry, she had proven leadership skills and was excited to be taking on her first business profit and loss account.

The business was stable, but to achieve her objectives, she knew she had to consider how to engage her staff and manage their performance. Tess said, "In a regulated environment like this, reporting and metrics are never going to go away. The question is how we use those metrics to engage people to deliver better outputs." Tess' core belief was that metrics stifle innovation and new ways of operating when they're set by senior leaders or come from the top. "When it comes to engagement and innovation," she explained, "the success of metrics comes down to how you create them, how you develop the targets. They have to come from the bottom up."

Tess recognised metrics risked acting as a de-motivator unless they were introduced at the right time, in the right way. She needed her team to reset, then ignite their seeking systems *before* she started talking about metrics. Tess began by taking the entire team, in multiple trips by the busload, to a football field where she had set up stalls around the stadium. In these stalls, team members could learn about the challenges and possibilities with robotics and AI fundamentals, information necessary for the digital overhaul

DOI: 10.4324/9781003396833-15

Tess was looking for. Employees gained some space to think, talk about, and reflect on how their jobs might be changed by digital, and how customer expectations were changing. Over the next week, each person helped create a new vision for what the organisation could become in the light of technology and digital advances, and how their work personally connected to that vision.

From there, the group created goals they could track with specific metrics. These metrics helped show them whether or not they were moving further toward their goals and vision. As a way to stay on track, individuals set their own targets. (Some leaders actually wanted to make the targets easier than the employees had suggested because they didn't believe they were achievable.) In just over three years, they had reduced costs by 40 percent – largely due to robotics and digital – while maintaining the book of insurance policies the company had written.

Tess' approach is a prime example of taking one aspect of a typical performance management process – in this case target setting – and tweaking it in a way that fuelled, rather than dampened, the seeking system. The core purpose of any performance management process is to enable individuals and teams to perform at their best so they can achieve individual and organisational success. However, most processes were originally built for predictable environments. They also often place more emphasis on *assessing* performance – for the calculation and distribution of compensation, promotions, and the like – than actually *improving* it.

Performance targets are such an entrenched feature within most organisations they become an assumption. Most managers can't envision managing performance without them, but then are frustrated when their employees do not contribute innovations, help the organisation adapt and learn, or get excited about finding new ways to compete. Leaders know they need their employees to be curious and enthusiastic, but they don't recognise how targets and metrics are shutting off the neurological systems that produce curiosity and enthusiasm in the first place. Current performance management practices tend to deactivate, not activate, the seeking system. They conflate multiple processes which, seen through the lens of the seeking system, actually work in direct opposition to each other and undermine that goal. For example, a meaningful coaching conversation with your line manager that gives you actionable insights to help you grow and improve can fuel the seeking system; being told you are rated as a "3" on a 1–5 scale at the end of a performance year will likely not.

Once we acknowledge the conflict between many performance systems and the seeking system, we then need a new way forward, a workable approach that lets us maintain an acceptable level of fairness and consistency while raising motivation and performance. In order to scale, alignment between employees is still necessary, and people must continue to get feedback on what is working and what is not. Tess McGregor found an approach to target setting that linked directly to an inspiring vision for the organisation. We need whole performance management systems that can do the same, working *with* leaders and team members' seeking systems – not against them. The end goal is to shift from managing performance to *inspiring* performance.

More Carrot, Less Stick

Performance management systems typically include both intrinsic and extrinsic motivators. Extrinsic motivation relies on social and monetary pressure; intrinsic motivation seeks to encourage employees through the promise of personal growth, autonomy, identity, common purpose, and social connection. Extrinsic motivation actually reduces intrinsic motivation by "crowding it out." If working harder at something that people already know how to do is the desired behaviour, then extrinsic motivators have a place in performance management approaches. But if companies want employees to work smarter, demonstrating innovative and adaptive behaviours in service of the organisation's purpose, then intrinsic motivation becomes more critical.

Formal performance management processes typically emerge as organisations grow and decide they need more structure for consistency, transparency, and fairness in their treatment of employees. The process may include prescriptive rules (and extensive documentation) for setting objectives, conducting performance evaluations, and rating employees against preset criteria, often at set times during the year. They regularly lead to a gated approach to progression, with promotions only happening on an annual or biannual cycle. To fuel the seeking system, the emphasis must be shifted away from this formal process.

Reviews of research on both performance appraisal and performance management have shown little if any evidence that current performance management systems have any real impact on the actual performance or effectiveness of employees.[1] The main reason for this ineffectiveness appears to be the conflicting objectives and multiple trade-offs inherent in the system. A rating system can make compensation decisions much easier, but it may demotivate more managers and employees than it inspires; extrinsic motivation increases effort, and individual performance metrics makes it easier rank performance, but hard metrics may encourage internal competition and unethical behaviours. More than a century of research has been devoted to identifying and fixing the problems with performance appraisal and performance management systems in organisations, but to date, this research has not led to the development of an approach that is seen by their users as consistently accurate, motivating, or useful.

So, what to do? Each core component of performance management must be redesigned in a way that fuels, rather than dampens, the seeking system. The mnemonic CARROT can be used to describe the most critical aspects:

- **C**ontinuous coaching
- **A**ssess with judgement, not numbers
- **R**eward teams, reduce contingent pay
- **R**ecognise effort & behaviours
- **O**bjectives to promote learning
- **T**arget more measures (and less targets)

Continuous Coaching

Coaching is the most important part of any performance management approach – and the easiest to get wrong. At its most basic, coaching is a process in which line managers seek to improve employees' performance through discussions about their past performance and future challenges. Managers typically collect employees' performance information and then provide them with feedback and advice on what they can do better. Simple as it may sound, in recent years, coaching has had a greater impact on the fear system than the seeking system.

To better understand why, let's examine the common characteristics of coaching conversations, as shown in the following table. Some of the activities will activate the fear system, and others the seeking system. In looking at the table, which attributes do you recognise, and which don't seem familiar at your organisation? What elements are part of your current performance management system? Are your coaching conversations activating employees' fear systems or seeking systems?

Characteristics of Coaching Conversations	Fear System Activation	Seeking System Activation
Mindset	• Holding employees accountable • Parent to child	• Developing employees • Adult to adult
Focus	• Identifying weaknesses that can be improved • Focusing on outcomes	• Building on strengths; using strengths to address development needs • Focusing on learning and skills acquisition
Frequency	• Annual review meeting	• Continuous conversation following the natural cycle of work, such as when a project finishes, a milestone is reached, a challenge pops up, etc.
Responsibility	• Conversation set up by manager	• Conversation set up by either employee or manager if an opportunity is seen for growth
Feedback	• Manager to employee	• Networked
Link to assessment & reward	• All feedback is an "assessment" with an implied link to compensation	• Assessment only for development and de-coupled from compensation
Emotional state	• Anxiety	• Focused Curiosity

There has been a shift over the years away from the annual performance review meetings and towards more frequent, ongoing, coaching dialogue between line manager and employee. Many organisations have reported the benefits of this shift. But effective coaching that activates and fuels the seeking system is about more than just having frequent conversations with employees and discussing work tasks. The goal of a coaching relationship between a leader and an employee is to shift from a corporate, procedural system to one that feels more caring and human.

Coaching conversations and interactions must therefore take a different approach, where personal accountability for performance is emphasised over managers holding their direct reports accountable. These conversations need to be more than just a box to be checked and must be held in a safe and honest environment. They must also be held at a frequency that allows a trusting working relationship to develop. Whilst the frequency, length, and format of these conversations is highly role- and individual-dependent, as a rule-of-thumb never let it go longer than two weeks without a check-in.

This approach highlights an important truth about performance management – it is the quality of the relationship between line manager and employee that really matters the most. Highly structured processes can actually reduce line manager accountability for this relationship as the focus becomes completion of the process. Here's an example of how they could look.

A Coaching Conversation to Fuel the Seeking System

John has just finished a major project that took nearly six months, a huge portion of his working year. He is ambitious, and keen to get some candid feedback on his overall performance. Though he has been having weekly coaching conversations with his line manager to discuss his immediate performance and help him address challenges, he now wants a broader career discussion. John feels accountable for his performance and career, and he takes the responsibility for convening the meeting.

John wants to take on more responsibility and is hoping to get promoted within a year. He wants to know whether he is on track and what else he needs to do to achieve this goal. His manager, Sally, starts the conversation by clarifying objectives and ground rules. This "contracting" portion of the conversation helps aligns the two participants' expectations[2] by agreeing on what John hopes to get out of the meeting and both his and Sally's roles in achieving it. This part of the discussion also provides an opportunity to reinforce that the meeting is focused on development, not assessment for promotion or compensation, which can take place separately.

Next, Sally asks John about his life goals. By transcending the job and connecting with John at the level of life goals – not just career goals – she is better equipped to help him as a person, not just an employee.[3] She says, "Imagine it's ten years from now and there's a party celebrating you and your accomplishments . . . Who is there? And what is the accomplishment everyone is there to celebrate?" She then works backward to what a five-year, three-year, and one-year goal would be to get John closer to that vision. The conversation helps to focus John on the skills he is acquiring now and how they will help him have his best impact on the world. Getting promoted is still highly relevant, but it is an outcome of obtaining and practicing these skills he needs to achieve his purpose.

Then Sally turns to the last six months and asks John to describe the skills needed to be exceptional in his role over that time period. After John lists them off, Sally asks him to self-assess his own skill levels against those he just named. John has previously received candid feedback from not only Sally but also his wider network throughout the project, so it's fairly easy for him to make a rounded assessment of his own skills. He identifies whether he is still learning the skill, he has mastered it, or if he is now actively teaching it to others. Sally asks which of these skills represents his particular strengths and how he has deployed those during the project. (Such self-expression and self-affirmation of strengths can help to restore a person's self-regard when they feel vulnerable,[4] while also making them feel more committed to the organisation.) John has completed a "Highlights Reel," as described in Chapter 7, and describes how he has sought to bring more of his strengths into his day-to-day work. Sally and John explore ways in which John could craft his time, tasks, and relationships, or rethink how he thinks about them, to further increase his impact at work.

This leads into a discussion about further skills development. Sally and John talk about the skills he would need if he were promoted, and compares those to his current assessment as well. Staying with strengths, they then explore how he can use his strengths to address current skills gaps, and they make a plan of action: John will construct one short-term and one long-term business challenge to ignite his seeking system. Next, Sally takes the perspective of "the eyes and voice of the business" to affirm, modify, or push back on John's challenges. The meeting concludes with John having greater clarity on his strengths and how he can use them to develop the skills needed to achieve his ambition. By decoupling the conversation from rewards, the conversation focuses on John's growth and the excitement of meeting those challenges, which fuels his seeking system.

No matter what leader handles this type conversation, the purpose is always the same – to help employees be the best they can be. Though there is clear evidence that employee coaching can be effective to this end,[5] it is also clear that there are significant challenges to effective coaching. As a coach, you are most likely to succeed if you are willing to communicate honestly with employees about their performance and remain open to learning. You will improve with practice when you are willing to work with employees and believe they can improve. When you and other managers work toward developing the skills to have these types of conversations, you'll build trust and better relationships, and help to fuel the seeking systems of all your employees.

Assess with Judgement, Not Numbers

It is helpful to make the distinction between the two separate functions assessment can fulfil. First, there is *assessment for development*. This type of assessment is detailed in the coaching section above, in which leaders provide performance information and feedback in service of employee improvement. The second type is *assessment for consequences*. This type of assessment enables the business to make decisions about rewards and sanctions. While they serve different purposes, the two assessment conversations are often conflated, which diminishes their effectiveness. It is difficult to have a meaningful development conversation while feeling the anxiety of being given a rating that impacts your pay. For 50 years, researchers have advocated separating the two – but organisations have found it difficult to do in practice.

Many leaders consider assessment to be more than a mechanism to fairly distribute reward – they consider it as a major (if not *the* major) motivational device to drive better performance. The thinking goes that employees will be inspired when they know they are performing better than most of their peers, or they will be motivated to work harder if they rank lower – especially if there is a clear link between their assessment and their reward. This assumption can be true, at least for some, when employees know exactly what they need to do to achieve their goals. Under those circumstances, the social and economic pressure provided by knowing how you rate against your peers can focus people and make them work harder and achieve better performance in the short term.

Unfortunately, that pressure dampens the seeking system and can be destructive when people are unsure of what they need to do to succeed.[6] When people need to innovate and practice new behaviours, the anxiety caused by ratings and other forms of assessment can lead to significantly less agility and adaptability. For many years the research has been pretty unanimous: if your business needs to adapt and change frequently to stay competitive, performance ratings make actual performance drop.[7]

With this realisation, many large organisations have already abandoned or substantially curtailed their use of formal performance appraisal systems, including Deloitte, Microsoft, and Adobe – and others have followed suit. In 2014, management research firm CEB (now Gartner) estimated that 12 per-cent of US companies had dropped annual reviews altogether, and the trend has continued to accelerate. Replacing annual reviews with ongoing coach-ing conversations, and "going numberless" by dropping rankings, certainly supports continual fuelling of the seeking system, but decisions about pay and promotions still have to be made. So employee contributions need to be assessed in some way. How can you, as a leader, make fair, meaningful assessments without causing the anxiety of social comparison or taking up too much of your managerial time?

The trade-offs that abound in performance management mean that any approach will have pitfalls, and you need to experiment with the specific approach that works best for your business. The following suggestions, how-ever, should enable assessments while maintaining fuelled seeking systems:

- Use ongoing coaching, as described, to provide meaningful assessment for development. Remember, great performance is a function of a great relationship between leaders and employees.
- When it comes to assessment for consequences, go numberless. Don't use or communicate ratings or attempt to use relative performance as a motivation device. An algorithm will never be as accurate or nuanced as a close working knowledge of each employee and their strengths, devel-opment needs, and performance against objectives.
- Rely on expert judgement, but to reduce bias when making an assess-ment, ask the below questions about each employee. Use these ques-tions several times per year so they fit into the natural cycle of work and refer to these "micro assessments" when making decisions about pay or promotion. Then discuss them with your employee. Make this conversa-tion separate from the ongoing coaching for development meetings:
  - If it were my own money, would I award this person the highest pos-sible compensation increases and bonuses? Why or why not?
  - Given everything I know of this person's performance, would I always want him or her on my team? Why or why not?
  - Is this person at risk for low performance? Would I prefer it if they joined my competitor?
  - Is this person ready for promotion today? What am I waiting for?

- Identify the top and bottom 10 percent of performers, as they will require interventions beyond the day-to-day coaching from their line managers (for example, high potential programs, promotion processes, or performance improvement plans). Don't spend time calibrating the middle 80 percent, as this takes a huge amount of time and effort for very limited return. Avoid the dark side of transparency – never share relative performance with employees, except those being promoted or managed for poor performance.
- Assessment should be conducted by the managers who have a coaching relationship with the employees or who otherwise work closely with them and know them well.

The very concept of assessment for consequences is tailor made to dampen employees' seeking systems. When ratings and social comparisons are removed, however, and a healthy ongoing coaching relationship flourishes, employees can become more engaged and focused on their own growth, fuelling the seeking system for the long term.

Reward Teams, Reduce Contingent Pay

The rewards employees receive can be roughly split into two categories: tangible and intangible. Tangible rewards include base pay, contingent pay, bonuses, and any long-term incentives, as well as pensions, holidays, healthcare, and other benefits. Intangible rewards include workplace learning, career development, supportive work environments, and interesting and inspiring work. When it comes to seeking system activation, the focus should be on maximising intangible rewards, while attempting to prevent tangible rewards from becoming salient, that is, the main motivator for work. This can be challenging for many organisations, especially because of a fixation on the single biggest dampener of seeking system activation: contingent pay, otherwise known as "pay for performance."

Pay for performance sounds logical: employees should give greater effort if the results of that effort are tied directly to greater levels of compensation. The trouble is that years of research have demonstrated that this is rarely the case. Pay-for-performance systems crowd out seeking system activation. Creativity and problem solving are subsumed by a focus on making numbers or getting visibility, and this can lead to, at best, a reduction in long-term performance, if not something much more catastrophic.

Wells Fargo, the US retail bank, determined that they needed to increase "cross selling" in order to improve their performance. To do so, the bank set quotas for employees to sign up customers for additional products and services. Failure to reach the quota resulted in having to work additional hours without pay until the quotas were hit, or the threat of termination. In response, large numbers of employees started to create PIN numbers to enrol customers in new services without informing them. The scale of the fraud was extensive and was a predictable response to the system. Needless to say, Wells Fargo suffered massive financial and reputational losses after news of the fraud broke in September 2016.

Pay for performance even affects the highest-income individuals, who would ostensibly experience the least financial threat. Studies have shown that paying CEOs based on stock options significantly increases the likelihood of earnings manipulations, shareholder lawsuits, and product safety problems. When people's remuneration depends on a specific measurement, they generally maximise their performance on that measurement alone, regardless of the wider systemic consequences.

So, when it comes to rewards, the biggest impact you could have on seeking system activation would be to abolish pay for performance. Surely, some of you are thinking "fat chance!" But it can be done, and the results can lead to higher performance. Professor Roger Martin, former dean of the Rotman School of Management at the University of Toronto, reports that New York corporate Law Firm Cravath, Swaine & Moore, has zero pay for performance.[8] All partners get paid the same as others of equal partnership tenure in what is called the Cravath scale. The firm considers cooperation among partners the key to the best client service and long-term performance. They determined that pay for performance actually encouraged individualism over cooperation, along with incentives to game the system, and therefore did away with it. Combined with a specific focus on non-tangible rewards, such as a pleasant and cooperative work environment, their approach enables them to both be financially successful and to attract and retain the best partners.

Complete abolition of pay for performance may be too radical for some, but its worst effects on dampening the seeking system can also be mitigated through other means, including team, as compared to individual, rewards. A 2013 meta-analysis of team versus individual financial incentives[9] demonstrates the importance of rewarding employees as teams to motivate them to a greater extent. Still, a mixture of team and individual rewards is necessary.

Individuals are motivated by personal growth, which should be encouraged, plus it's important to avoid instances of "social loafing," where a successful team effectively carries a lower performing team member.

Somewhat paradoxically, when it comes to keeping the seeking system fuelled, it can also help to keep reward decisions opaque. Transparency among employees receiving higher, lower, or different rewards can result in reduced overall engagement for all but those deemed the highest performers. Indeed, in one organisation the introduction of a clear rewards process increased the transparency around bonus allocation by 17 percent but reduced overall trust in the organisation by 7 percent and the perception of fairness of rewards relative to job effort by 8 percent.[10]

Pay raises, promotions, and bonuses need to be tied to the performance of the whole business or unit and then allocated at the discretion of line managers. Remember, it is the line manager who is accountable for leading the performance of his or her team. Managers who ignite more of their team members' seeking systems will likely gain a greater share of rewards to distribute. Because an opaque approach using judgement is open to allegations of insufficient transparency and objectivity, companies need to counter the perception of unfairness by establishing systems that allow employees to provide feedback or challenge decisions. Companies such as Accenture and Lloyds Banking Group are finding that, when combined with more frequent coaching conversations, this discretionary approach results in fewer allegations of lack of fairness than the more traditional systems where ratings are linked directly to reward.

Recognise Effort and Behaviours

When we receive praise and affirmation from our colleagues, it satisfies a fundamental social need to feel like a valued member of a tribe. Recognition makes us feel secure, enhances our sense of belonging, and when done right, can be a powerful source of fuel for the seeking system. As "herd animals," our brains are hardwired to keep us safe within our social groups. Matt Lieberman at UCLA has shown in lab studies that the experience of social exclusion activates the same regions within the brain as those activated when a person experiences physical pain.[11] The mere prospect of social exclusion from a group can therefore be felt as keenly as physical pain.

The opposite is also true. Our seeking systems are fuelled when we are recognised as a valued member of our teams, especially when that recognition comes from people who have an influence on our security within our teams. Therefore, the most valued recognition comes from our organisational and group leaders, as well as from people in our immediate teams. Even when we receive recognition from these sources, a common problem may still occur.

We often place too much emphasis on recognising goal achievement, and too little on recognising effort, behaviours, learning, or progress. Recognition often comes in the form of "celebrating success" after, say, winning a new piece of business, delivering a great presentation, or completing a project. These successes usually come with their own reward systems, as we feel pride in what we have accomplished. But as a leader, your recognition can be more valuable *before* a goal is achieved, because it helps fuel employees' seeking systems throughout their work, resulting in enthusiasm and persistence that ultimately makes success more likely.

To become more practiced at recognising *progress* towards goals, try to reframe work as a learning opportunity. Offer praise and celebration at every possible point of "early wins." This type of encouragement is needed to accelerate learning, and your recognition will work best when it is frequent, and focused on effort, relevant behaviours, and small milestones. Many organisational leaders seek to achieve this by anchoring their recognition schemes on the demonstration of company values. This approach is useful as it focuses on desired behaviours rather than goal achievement. Just make sure that you recognise people for displaying the behaviours that reflect the values of your organisation.

Many businesses deploy formal recognition schemes supported by technology. Employees can recognise their colleagues for a particular behaviour that aligns to one of the company values by writing a few words about what their colleague said or did that they appreciated, then issuing them reward points via their laptops or mobile devices. Employees are given a finite number of points every month which they can distribute to colleagues they wish to recognise. Often, the points can be redeemed for low-value gift items via the platform.

Many such programs provide small extrinsic rewards as part of their recognition schemes, although the impact of the physical reward relative to the social reward of public recognition is debatable. What is more important is that your approach to recognition is aligned with your organisation's culture. For example, Missguided, the online fashion store, recognises employees by allowing them a spin of the "happiness wheel." Like the wheel of fortune, the employees win prizes, but these are playful and have low extrinsic value such as "the boss makes me coffee for a week." Charles Tyrwhitt, the tailor, issues values e-cards to employees; Kid Zania, the online game producer, values badges; Impraise, an online platform for managers, values trophies.

Objectives to Promote Learning

Objectives are goals that employees work toward. As a general principle, objectives should strike the right balance between a challenge ("I feel stretched") and competence ("I can do this") to keep the seeking system fuelled and maximise performance. If skills exceed the challenge presented by the objective, the individual or team will become bored and will not achieve the required level of performance. Similarly, if the challenge level exceeds the skills of the individual or team, anxiety can cripple performance. The optimum zone – the performance channel – keeps these two forces in balance, stretching and motivating employees without inducing anxiety or boredom. Finding this performance channel requires a close relation-ship between leaders and their employees, one that can be best achieved through the regular coaching conversations discussed earlier. When setting objectives that help employees stay within the performance channel, two elements need to be considered: the type of objectives being set and the way they are agreed to.

Setting Objectives

Objectives are typically cascaded through an organisation to provide a line of sight between the main objectives of the business, the team, and ulti-mately the individual. This strategy has many upsides, not least that indi-viduals understand how their own objectives contribute to a wider whole. Typically, these cascaded objectives are framed around achievement of some performance standard (for instance, have the highest profitability in the industry or increase market share by 20 percent). The knowledge and behaviours required to achieve these objectives, however, are not typically discussed as part of the objective setting process.

In order to fuel the seeking system, a new line of sight is required, as shown in Figure 10.1. In this case, team and individual performance objectives are broken down into behavioural objectives (the macro-level behaviours that lead to achievement of the performance goal) and learning

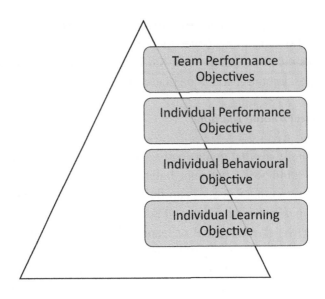

Figure 10.1
Performance Objectives Line of Sight

objectives (the skills and knowledge required to complete the tasks that meet the performance objective).

Individual performance objectives can be the most threatening to employees and dampen the seeking system. But that threat can be countered by providing a line of sight, and setting specific objectives for, individual behaviour and learning goals and team performance goals. As discussed in Chapter 5, learning goals can help to ignite the seeking system through a focus on growth and obtaining new insights. Only once an employee has the knowledge and behavioural skills necessary to perform the task will a performance objective provide the motivation of effort and persistence required to achieve it.

Start by exploring team and individual performance objectives with your employees, and gauge whether they are set at the right skills and challenge levels to put them in the performance channel. Then move onto behavioural and learning objectives, setting measurable goals for each. The greater the anxiety caused by the performance objectives, the greater you should focus on learning objectives to drive performance. The more you focus on learning objectives, the more you foster an adaptable, agile workforce. Research shows that learning objectives focus people on becoming competent, whereas performance objectives focus people on the *appearance* of competence.[12] Thus, the more you invest in helping your people learn and develop, the more you create the right processes to reward, recognise, and motivate employees who go the extra mile.

Agreeing to Objectives

Objectives imposed top down rarely fuel the seeking system. Setting goals for others not only reduces their sense of autonomy, but it's also easy to think that they are "just like you" and will have the same level of motivation for the objective in place. Of course, that's not always the case. A framework must therefore be created for employees to set objectives for themselves. One strong approach to do so can be broken down into the following four steps.

Step One

As part of a regular coaching conversation, ask employees to discuss a long-term future for the organisation that they find inspiring. Have them describe how meeting the team's performance objectives will help realise that vision.

Step Two

Ask employees to construct two to three individual performance objectives that will contribute to the achievement of the team performance objectives. These should be framed as the promises the individual is making to the team based on what they see as their main contributions to the team's success. These individual objectives represent the "how" of the team objectives – when completed, each of the individual "hows" should help to achieve the overall team objectives.

Step Three

Next, take the perspective of "the eyes and voice of the business" to affirm, modify, or push back on the employees' individual objectives, while keeping an open mind as to where you might be wrong. Continue the conversation until you and the team member reach agreement.

Step Four

Now invite the employees to set two to three specific behaviour and learning objectives that will be needed to achieve the individual performance objectives. (These should also be negotiated as described in steps one through three.) Make each of the objectives FAST: Goals should be embedded in *frequent* discussions; *ambitious* in scope; measured by *specific* metrics and milestones; and *transparent* for everyone in the organisation to see.

The metrics and milestones identified become targets for the individual and, as we shall see, targets need to be treated carefully.

Target More Measures (and Fewer Targets)

Economist Charles Goodhart[13] said that "Any measure used for control is unreliable" because "when a measure becomes a target, it ceases to become a good measure." This is because when targets lead to reward or punishment, they create threat and will be gamed to relieve the threat. The outcome? Disengagement of the seeking system and a focus on short-term goals above sustainable long-term purpose, such as shown in the Wells Fargo example earlier in the chapter. To fuel the seeking system, fear inducing targets must be made "non-salient." The following strategies can help you in that process.

Aim Off

Aiming off is a navigational strategy often used when hiking through wilderness areas with a map and compass. In aiming off, rather than taking a direct route to the target and potentially missing it, the hiker heads to a line feature near the target, such as a stream or wall, which then helps guide the way to the destination. This technique is safe, saves time, and maximises the chances of reaching the target.

To reduce the salience of performance targets, consider setting and tracking targets that may relate only obliquely to the performance goals. In practice, this means using targets sparingly, again focusing more on learning and behavioural targets than performance ones. Aim for a ratio of three learning and behavioural targets to every one performance target. (This ratio reflects work by Barbara Fredrickson, the Kenan Distinguished Professor of Psychology, at the University of North Carolina at Chapel Hill, who identified that three positive interactions are needed to counteract the effect of one negative interaction.)

Focus on Measures Over Targets

When Charles Goodhart showed that "when a measure becomes a target, it ceases to become a good measure" an obvious solution emerged: have more measures, and fewer targets. A large recruitment firm introduced aiming-off by having an enhanced, human experience for their clients and candidates as their primary goal, with profit being a consequence of this strategy.

Being offered and starting a new job is a significant moment in most people's lives, especially when employees can personally connect with the meaning in their work. Making that experience a delight for clients and candidates not only felt like a worthy purpose, but it made good business sense – candidates, clients, and employees would never forget a successful placement, making them more committed to the firm.

In order for employees to deliver on their personal sense of purpose with their work, they needed to understand how candidates and clients felt at every stage of their journey. Detailed journey maps became an imperative, and leaders worked with consultants to create customer surveys. They then ran analytics to learn the best drivers of delight at each stage. The metrics were made available to help employees deliver and test whether new initiatives were improving satisfaction or lowering it, but leaders never set targets. When a metric showed a dip in satisfaction scores, follow-up conversations and "importance analysis" of predictor variables would reveal why, and employees could immediately trial corrective action.

For example, when candidates showed lower satisfaction after an initial interview, analysis revealed that they felt they were leaving without all the information they wanted about the role they were interested in. Consultants then started to ask all candidates at the end of the interview, "Do you have any questions left?" This simple intervention increased interview satisfaction by 12%.

Since no target was placed on these metrics, there was no sense of threat or anxiety, which could have led employees to game the numbers. However, helping employees personalise the purpose of the work, and then aligning the metrics to that purpose, meant that the metrics were intrinsically interesting to employees. By making the data available to employees, they could identify areas for improvement and experiment with immediate changes to their working practices. This approach fuelled the seeking system rather than shut it off, and it also motivated employees since they knew it would help them achieve their purpose.

Summary

- The core purpose of any performance management process is to enable individuals and teams to perform at their best so they can achieve individual and organisational success. However, current management performance practices tend to deactivate, not activate, the seeking system. To fuel the seeking system, a new approach to performance management is needed.
- Each core component of performance management must be redesigned in a way that fuels, rather than dampens, the seeking system. Trade-offs abound and there is no one-size fits all solution.
- A performance management approach that fuels the seeking system may have some or all of the following CARROT characteristics:
    - **Continuous coaching**: conversations between line manager and employees focused on development, rather than annual reviews.
    - **Assess with judgment, not numbers**: assessment for development discussions decoupled from compensation discussions. When it comes to assessment for consequences (e.g., bonus, promotions, sanctions), go numberless. Don't use or communicate ratings or attempt to use relative performance as a motivation device. Instead, rely on expert judgement. To reduce potential bias, ask three or four critical questions about each employee.
    - **Reward teams, reduce contingent pay**: maximise intangible rewards such as opportunities for growth, while making tangible rewards "non salient." To do this, remove pay for performance and include team rewards.
    - **Recognise effort and behaviours**: the most valued recognition comes from people in our immediate teams, so set up systems for employee-to-employee recognition. Recognition works best when it is frequent and focused on effort, relevant behaviours, and small milestones, rather than big achievements.
    - **Objectives to promote learning:** objectives should focus on a new "line of sight," one in which performance objectives are linked to the behavioural and learning objectives required to achieve the performance outcome.
    - **Target more measures (and fewer targets):** when a measure becomes a target, it ceases to become a good measure. So have more measures, and fewer targets. Measures should be numerous enough to reflect the purpose of the work unit and updated frequently, ideally in "real time," to show rapid feedback on progress.

Notes

1　Performance Evaluation will not die, but it should. Provocation Paper, Human Resources Management Journal, August 2019.

2　Bennett, John L. (2008) "Contracting for success." *International Journal of Coaching in Organisations* 6(4): 7–14.

3　Evanish, J. (2012) *How to Help Your Team Achieve Their Goals.* CEO Get Lighthouse, Inc. https://getlighthouse.com/blog/how-team-achieve-goals/

4　Cohen, G. L., and D. K. Sherman (2014) "The psychology of change: self-affirmation and social psychological intervention." *The Annual Review of Psychology* 65: 333–371.

5　Gregory, Jane Brodie (2010) "Employee coaching relationships: enhancing construct clarity and measurement." *Coaching An International Journal of Theory Research and Practice* 3(2): 109–123.

6　Cappelli, Peter, and Anna Travis (2016, October) "The performance management revolution." *Harvard Business Review.* hbr.org.

7　Smith, B., J.S. Hornsby, and R. Shirmeyer (1996) "Current trends in performance appraisal: an examination of managerial practice." *SAM Advanced Management Journal* 61: 10–15.

8　It's Time to Accept that Pay for Performance Doesn't Work | by Roger Martin | Medium.

9　The effect of financial incentives on performance: A quantitative review of individual and team-based financial incentives Yvonne Garbers, Udo Konradt, First published: 05 October 2013.

10　Birkinshaw, Julian, and Dan Cable (2017, February 1) "The dark side of transparency." *McKinsey & Company.* mckinsey.com.

11　Eisenberger, Naomi I., et al. (2003) "Does rejection hurt? An fMRI study of social exclusion." *Science* 302: 290.

12　Rawsthorne, Laird J., and Andrew J. Elliot (1999) "Achievement goals and intrinsic motivation: a meta-analytic review." *Personality and Social Psychology Review* 3, no. 4: 326–344.

13　Goodhart, C.A.E. (1975) "Problems of monetary mangement: the UK experience." *Monetary Theory & Practice*: 91–121.

Conclusion

To create a vibrant organisation, leaders must help its people live their lives to the fullest. In return, the workforce becomes an enthusiastic volunteer army that works with conviction and creativity to solve the organisation's problems while improving team dynamics, retention rate, and employee satisfaction and health, as well as the organisation's bottom line.

I've been encouraged by the number of organisations that have started the journey of becoming more vibrant, which taps into deep human needs about how people want to live and work in the world today. Many popular movements share similar philosophies based on the simple idea that we can achieve more – as individuals, organisations, and societies – when we are truly connected to meaning, purpose, and actions that give us fulfilment. Conscious capitalism, the B Corp movement, and inclusive capitalism all share a desire for business to place social and environmental value on an equal footing with shareholder value by leading with purpose and passion. Similarly, the positive psychology movement has created legions of followers since Martin Seligman first began pioneering and popularising the topic more than 20 years ago. Many organisations now use positive and appreciative methods to address the challenges of change, leadership development, creativity, and improved group dynamics. These methods nurture flourishing organisations while dealing with the issues at hand.

Despite these encouraging developments, problems with *scaling* the enthusiasm needed for a fully vibrant organisation still exist. Individuals and teams may experience moments of seeking system activation, but these continue to be dampened by organisational systems and behaviours that value control and predictability over inspiration and creativity. This presents a still untapped opportunity for organisations to embrace the strategies and tools in this book to create vibrant organisations for the long term.

My hope is that this book will act as a guide for those willing to embark on that journey. The practical strategies and tools included in these pages are based on some essential and sometimes surprising science about creating an emotional transformation of your workforce. This means that to create vibrant organisations, leaders will have to let go of a number of established orthodoxies.

To start, leaders must develop an unfailing belief in human potential. They must cede control to the front line and encourage employees to explore, learn, and personalise their purpose. This means accepting that you don't have all the answers, or at least that better answers may exist if you give your people the opportunities to bring their best selves to work. Efficiency should also be subordinated to effectiveness when it comes to scaling. Emotions scale differently from ideas, and leaders should embrace emotional contagion above fully sequenced rollouts.

Enthusiasm is a fickle beast that requires constant attention. Leaders should start by activating their own seeking systems, experimenting with some of the strategies in this book, and utilising their own unique gifts in service of their personal and organisational purpose. With their own seeking systems activated, leaders can then help others by facilitating self-directed neuroplasticity, continually focusing employees on the main triggers of the seeking system. To do this, they must repeat the three-step sequence that makes up the main structure of this book: reset, ignite, and fuel.

To reset means creating a safe environment for employees' self-expression, and to help them increase feelings of autonomy and control by providing freedom to operate within a clear and focused framework. To ignite at scale, leaders need to engineer experiences that provoke employees into flashes of insight that change their mental maps. This can include embedding a coaching culture and helping employees to use their strengths in service of the organisational culture. Fuel is about giving repeated attention to the new thought patterns in order for them to stay alive. By encouraging continued practice of new behaviours, introducing rituals at work, and making some radical changes to the way performance is managed, you can help ensure your team members' seeking systems stay fuelled for the long term. Understanding the science behind the strategies, tools, and ideas discussed throughout this book can better enable tweaks and changes to make the sequence work in your own context.

Activating the seeking system at scale creates a workforce who feel a zest for life and work, who are more resilient, work harder and longer on problems, and are significantly more innovative. You, your organisation, and the world need more of this. It's not easy, and there will be challenges throughout any activation journey. But you need to stay optimistic – idealistic even – and recognise there is a better way to work, a more satisfying way to make a living, and the ability to lead true change for the benefit of not just you and your people, but society as a whole. As you set out on this journey, feel free to reach out and share what you've learned, how you've been able to activate your teams' best selves, and where you've run into roadblocks along the way. My hope is that all of us, together, can push beyond the dreariness of workaday lives and create our own vibrant organisations.

Index

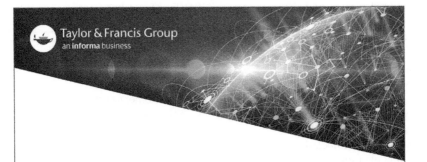